A CENTURY OF FASHIONS

DRESS PATTERN ILLUSTRATIONS, 1898-1997

Alice I. Duff

Schiffer Publishing Ltd

4880 Lower Valley Road · Atglen, Pennsylvania 19310

Schiffer Books are available at special discounts
for bulk purchases for sales promotions
or premiums. Special editions, including
personalized covers, corporate imprints, and
excerpts can be created in large quantities for
special needs. For more information contact the
publisher:

Published by Schiffer Publishing Ltd.
4880 Lower Valley Road
Atglen, PA 19310
Phone: 610-593-1777; Fax: 610-593-2002
E-mail: Info@schifferbooks.com

For the largest selection of fine reference
books on this and related subjects, please
visit our website at:
www.schifferbooks.com
We are always looking for people to write
books on new and related subjects. If you
have an idea for a book please contact us at
the above address.

This book may be purchased from the
publisher.
Include $5.00 for shipping.
Please try your bookstore first.
You may write for a free catalog.

In Europe, Schiffer books are distributed by
Bushwood Books
6 Marksbury Ave.
Kew Gardens
Surrey TW9 4JF England
Phone: 44 (0) 20 8392 8585; Fax: 44 (0) 20
8392 9876
E-mail: info@bushwoodbooks.co.uk
Website: www.bushwoodbooks.co.uk

Other Schiffer Books on Related Subjects:
Emerging Fashion Designers
978-0-7643-3600-3, $39.99

Emerging Fashion Designers 2
978-0-7643-3791-8, $39.99

ACKNOWLEDGMENT OF TRADEMARKS

"Ageless Patterns" is a registered trademark of Ageless Patterns, PO Box 1145, Tombstone, AZ 85638, 520-457-3241, www.agelesspatterns.com. Their use herein is for identification purposes only. All rights are reserved by owner.

The text and products pictured in this book are from the collection of the author of this book. This book is not sponsored, endorsed or otherwise affiliated with any of the companies whose products are represented herein. They include Decades of Style, Vintage Pattern Lending Library, and Ageless Patterns. This book is derived from the author's independent research.

Designed by RoS
Type set in Univers/Humanist521 BT
ISBN: 978-0-7643-3698-0
Printed in China

DEDICATION

In memory of Katlyn, a sweet cat.

ACKNOWLEDGMENTS

Thanks to my mother, Martha Duff, who gave me help all those years ago.

CONTENTS

INTRODUCTION

I started collecting dress patterns at about the age of 14, back in the 1970s, when they still could be bought for five or ten cents at the Salvation Army. When I was fifteen, for a school project, my mother made a dress for me from one of my 1940s patterns. I am not an expert sewer and to this day have not completed a garment from an old pattern.

Over the years, my collection grew so that now it exceeds 250 patterns and several pattern catalogs, ranging in date from 1898 to 1997. What is fascinating to me about pattern illustrations is that the drawings are in the style of the day, the image of the "ideal" body at that time. As we all know, styles changed dramatically throughout the twentieth century. I was very disappointed when pattern covers began having photographs of models instead of drawings; it's much harder to portray an ideal body style in a photograph than it is in a drawing.

A little history on patterns is in order. In the middle of the nineteenth century, shortly after Isaac Singer introduced the home sewing machine, Ellen and William Demorest invented the paper pattern. In 1863, Ebenezer Butterick patented and sold the first graded or sized paper pattern. At first, and for many years, patterns were perforated, not printed, and the accompanying instructions were minimal. To actually use a pattern one had to be generally familiar with how garments were constructed, and be better than a beginner. It would be more than fifty years before pattern companies would issue printed patterns and thus start catering to the beginning sewer. Nowadays, the instructions often are more bulky than the pattern!

The 30s, 40s and 50s of the last century were the heyday of dress patterns. There were many companies, including DuBarry, Hollywood, Pictorial Review, New York, Anne Adams, Marion Martin, May Manton and Modes Royal. Today, there are the "big four" — Butterick, McCall's, Simplicity, and Vogue — but there are also many small companies producing reproduction patterns. A few of these are included, as well as several "retro" patterns from the big four.

I have relied on my knowledge and intuition to arrange the patterns generally in chronological order, but some may be out of place. It is difficult to be precise as only McCall's consistently dated its patterns. Of course, fashions don't follow the calendar decades. For example, a pattern I have placed in the 1930-1939 chapter may actually have come out in 1940.

Sit back and enjoy this book as it explores a fascinating century of popular shapes and styles.

One
major
influence:
_____

World War I

C HAPTER O NE

Pre-1920

#1389 - $16.50

AGELESS PATTERNS ™©1999-2002
vintage reproduction patterns for theatrical costumers

1898 STRAWBERRY RED LINEN COSTUME
38 BUST   26 WAIST

NO RETURNS, EXCHANGES OR REFUNDS ON PATTERNS
FABRIC DEPOT, INC.

THE COSTUME ILLUSTRATED IS OF CRUSHED-STRAWBERRY-COLORED LINEN, EDGED WITH FOLDS OF WHITE, AND TRIMMED WITH SOME WHITE CORD EMBROIDERY ON THE FRONTS AND BACK OF THE JACKET AND AROUND THE BOTTOM OF THE SKIRT.

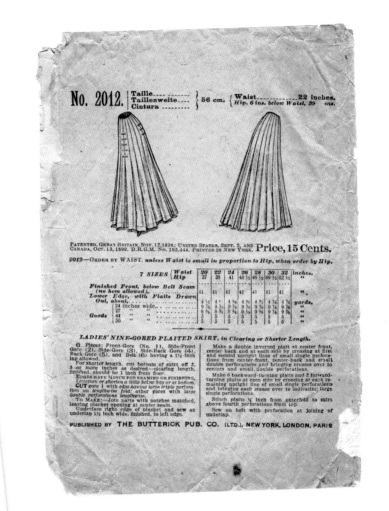

A circa 1898 retro pattern for theatrical costumers.

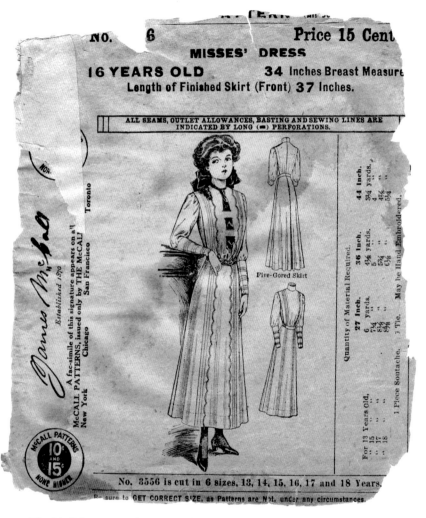

This McCall pattern is for a young lady. Notice the "S" curve in profile, even for a sixteen-year-old.

#1392 - $27.50

AGELESS PATTERNS™ ©1999-2002
vintage reproduction patterns for theatrical costumers

1898 ÉTAMINE GOWN W/INSERTIONS
38 BUST   26 INCHES

GRAY ÉTAMINE IS THE MATERIAL OF THIS GOWN, TRIM
WHICH ARE UNDERLAID WITH WHITE

#1642 - $28.25

AGELESS PATTERNS™ © 1999-2006
VICTORIAN REPRODUCTION PATTERNS - 1867 - 1917
"SEW AUTHENTIC"

1901 MOURNING DRESS
38 BUST   25 WAIST

THIS MOURNING DRESS OF BLACK WOOL POPLIN, DECORATED WITH ENGLISH CREPE
FABRIC, WITH THE SKIRT ENCIRCLED WITH TWO FLOUNCES OF CREPE EXCEPT THE
FRONT GORE WHICH IS COVERED WITH TWO LARGE BIAS STRIPS OF CREPE WHICH
REPRESENTS AN APON. ENGLISH TRANSLATION AND ORIGINAL FRENCH SEWING
INSTRUCTIONS INCLUDED.

COSMOPOLITAN FASHION MODEL ❧ CO. PAPER PATTERN

No seams allowed for on this Pattern

Quantity of 36 inch material

For 32 inches bust measure.... 2¾ yds

34	,,	,,	,, ... 2⅞
36	,,	,,	,, ... 3
38	,,	,,	,, ... 3⅛
40	,,	,,	,, ... 3¼

32 inches Bust Measure.

1900 Ladies' Waist.

This pattern consists of ten pieces: **Under Front, Outer Front, Under-arm Gore Yoke, Back, Collar, Upper and Under Sleeve portions, Cuff and Belt.** In cutting lay the edges marked by triple perforations on a length-wise fold of goods to avoid a seam. Join the parts according to corresponding notches. Take up the darts in front by meeting corresponding perforations and turn under the front edge on line of perforations for an inturn. Include the right side of outer front in shoulder and under-arm seam of under-waist and adjust the left side when worn.

Close seams of sleeve, gather on upper edge between the notches and fit to armscye with front seam at notch. Join cuff to lower edge of sleeve and collar to neck edge according to notches. If preferred the under fronts may be fastened on shoulder and under-arm seam. Place belt over lower edge of waist.

PRICE 25 CENTS.

Instructions printed on envelope.

#1652 - $23.75

AGELESS PATTERNS ™© 1999-2006

VICTORIAN REPRODUCTION PATTERNS - 1867 - 1917

"SEW AUTHENTIC"

1901 RED SERGE DRESS
38 BUST   25 WAIST

THIS DRESS IS MADE OF RED SERGE WITH WHITE PIPING, WORN WITH A WHITE LEATHER
BELT AND A SHIRT FRONT OR DICKEY OF CREAM COLOR STIPPLED WITH RED. ENGLISH
TRANSLATION AND ORIGINAL FRENCH SEWING INSTRUCTIONS INCLUDED.

2488

EARLY CENTURY

PRINCESS DRESS

Size 36 Bust

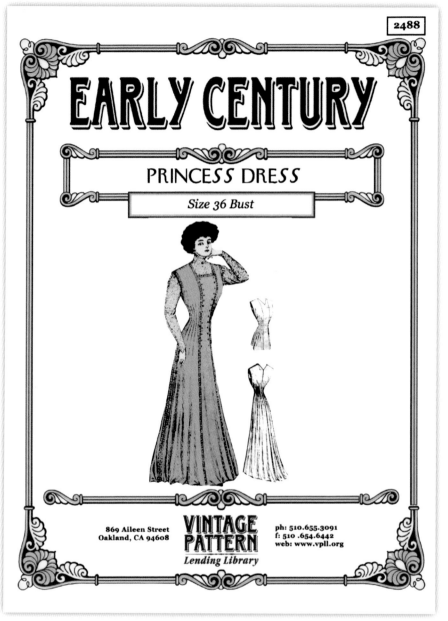

869 Aileen Street
Oakland, CA 94608

VINTAGE
PATTERN
Lending Library

ph: 510.655.3091
f: 510 .654.6442
web: www.vpll.org

A circa 1908 retro pattern.

MAY MANTON'S
BAZAR GLOVE-FITTING PATTERNS

Trademark   *May Manton*   Registered

ALLOW ALL SEAMS ON THIS PATTERN.

DIRECTIONS.—Lay all pieces on the cloth; trace around the outer edges and allow seams as material requires; baste on tracings. The different parts are notched to show how the pattern should be put together. The following symbols are used:

✛ One cross where garment is to be plaited.   ✛✛ Two crosses where garment is to be gathered.   ✛✛✛ Three crosses where there is no seam.

GUARANTEED A PERFECT FIT FOR A PERFECT FIGURE.

SIX-PIECE SKIRT

With Empire, High or Natural Waist Line.

Four-pieces.—Front Gore, Back Gore, Side-Front Gore, Side-Back Gore. The front gore is indicated by group of three large perforations.

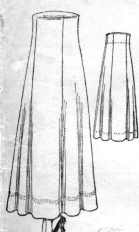

Lay edge of front and of back gore marked by triple crosses on lengthwise fold, line of perforations in each side gore lengthwise. **For high waist-line cut off on first line of perforations, for natural waist-line, cut off on second line of perforations from upper edge.** Join pieces by corresponding notches.

Join front and side-front, back and side-back gores, leaving opening at left side of back above notches, for placket. Underface right edge of opening. Finish left with underlap. Close side seams. **For Empire waistline, bone the seams and underface upper edges; for high waist-line,** arrange over webbing one and one-half inches in width; **for natural waistline,** underface or join to belt the size of waist.

8450A Six-Piece Skirt, 24 to 34 waist.

QUANTITY OF MATERIAL REQUIRED.
When Material has neither Figure nor Nap.

	27 in. wide.	36 in. wide.	44 or 54 in. wide.
Small.	8¼ yards.	4½ yards.	3⅜ yards.
Medium	8¼ "	4½ "	3⅜ "
Large.	8¾ "	4¾ "	3⅝ "

When Material has Figure or Naps.

	27 in. wide.	36 in. wide.	44 or 54 in. wide.
Small.	5½ yards.	3½ yards.	2⅞ yards.
Medium	5½ "	3½ "	2⅞ "
Large.	6 "	4 "	3⅛ "

Width of skirt at lower edge, 2 yards and 30 inches, for medium size.

8490A   32 Inches Waist   46 Inches Hip

ECONOMY PATTERN
—ALL SEAMS ALLOWED — SAVES TIME MONEY & MATERIAL —
— SPECIAL PRICE 6¢ MAILED — SEARS, ROEBUCK & CO.—

LADIES' APRON OR HOUSE DRESS, Closed at Left Side of Front. 7 Pieces. Front—marked 1 oblong —, Side-Front and Pocket—2 oblongs, Side-Back—3 oblongs, Back—4 oblongs, Sleeve and Sleeve Band.
Cut in sizes 32, 34, 36, 38, 40 and 42 inches bust measure.

YARDS OF MATERIAL REQUIRED.
Without up and down.

	27 ins.	36 ins.	44 ins	Insertion.
For 32 or 34 ins. bust	6	4¾	4	⅜
For 36 or 38 ins. bust	6½	5½	4⅛	⅜
For 40 or 42 ins. bust	7¼	6	4½	¾

DIRECTIONS FOR CUTTING AND MAKING

▶ **Match Notches** in closing seams.

○○ **Large Triple Perforations**—No Seam, lay on lengthwise fold.

●●● **Three Small Perforations**—Lay straight of goods.

○ **Single Large or** ○ **Small Perforations**—For tucks, plaits, etc.

○○ **Large Double Perforations**—Gatherings and Shirrings.

If any of the above marks are omitted, they are not needed for this pattern.
⅜ inch is allowed on all edges for seams.

All seams are allowed for.

5630

For low neck, cut neck edge out 1 inch. If necessary to change length, cut through pattern 3 inches above waistline notches and separate or lap—2½ inches are allowed for hem. Change sleeve at lower edge.

TO MAKE:—Sew a pocket to each side-front with double notches together and with upper back corner at large perforation. Close seams as notched, leaving left side-front seam loose for closing. Underface loose edge of front and sew an under lap to loose edge of side-front for closing with buttons and buttonholes.

SLEEVE:—Close seam and gather upper and lower edges between double perforations. Join ends of sleeveband and sew to sleeve with seams even. Sew in sleeve, placing large single perforation at shoulder seam.

5630 Price, 10 Cents   Bust Measure.

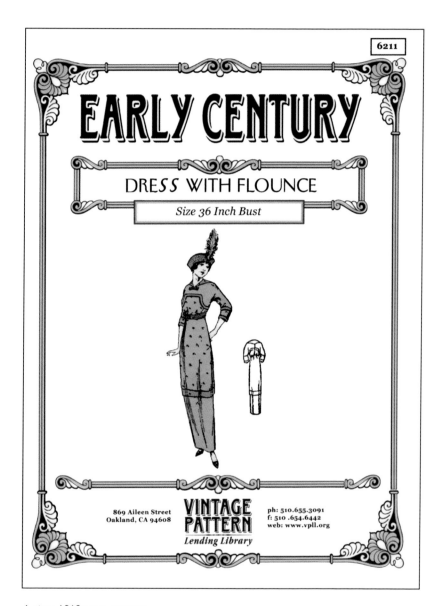

A circa 1912 retro pattern.

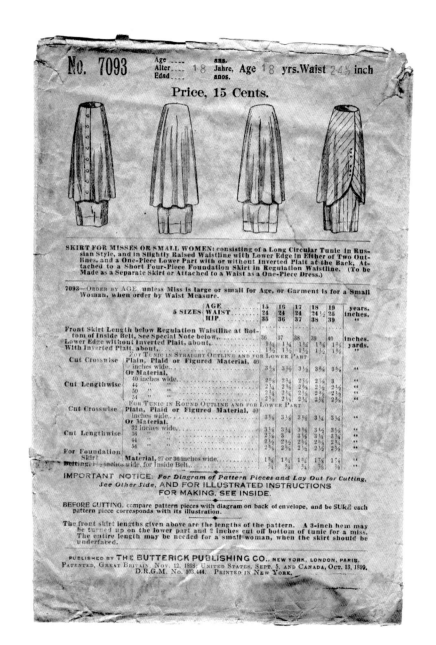

PUBLISHED BY THE BUTTERICK PUBLISHING CO., NEW YORK, LONDON, PARIS.
Patented, Great Britain, Nov. 12, 1895; United States, Sept. 5, and Canada, Oct. 13, 1899.
D.R.G.M. No. 103,444. Printed in New York.

No. **7198**   Size **40**   Price **15** Cents

RULES Don't remove the pattern from envelope until you have made sure it is the right size to use in Ladies' Home Journal Patterns, by measuring thus: Stand behind the person and place a tape around the form, close up under the arms; lower it in front so it passes over the fullest part of the bust; raise it in the back so it crosses the lower edges of the shoulder-blades; the measurement, in inches, is the size of pattern to use. If the size of this pattern is smaller than the form measures, take it back and exchange it. A pattern which is a trifle large can be fitted easily by taking up at the seams. Measure over the dress, and loosely unless a close fit is wanted. Never use a pattern smaller than the form measures.

View A

View C

View B

View B

View A

DESCRIPTION LADIES' AND MISSES' COAT, fastened to the neck, or turned back to form short or long revers, slightly enlarged armhole, set-in sleeve with turn-back cuff. Coat may be cut off for shorter length. Length of coat from neck at center-back, 54 inches, shorter length about 45 inches. For material required see table below.

View B in 54-inch Length		
Cut in 4 sizes	Without up and down 36 in. wide 42 in. wide	With up and down 54 in. wide
32	4¾ yards 4¼ yards	3½ yards
36	5¼ yards 4¾ yards	3¾ yards
40	6¾ yards 5 yards	4 yards
44	6 yards 5¼ yards	4 yards

View B in 45-inch Length: Size 36 requires 4 yards 42-inch material without up and down.

View A in 54-inch Length: Size 36 requires 3½ yards 42-inch material without up and down, with 1¼ yards 36-inch or wider contrasting material without up and down for collar, cuffs and revers facing.

View A in 45-inch Length: Size 36 requires 3 yards 42-inch material without up and down, with 1¼ yards 36-inch or wider contrasting material without up and down for collar, cuffs and revers facing.

This is a perfect pattern. See our guarantee on the flap of this envelope.

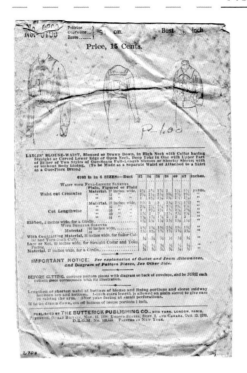

Price, 15 Cents.

LADIES' BLOUSE-WAIST, Bloused or Drawn Down, in High Neck with Collar having Straight or Curved Lower Edge or Open Neck, Deep Yoke in One with Upper Part of Either of Two Styles of One-Seam Full-Length Sleeves or Shorter Sleeve with or without Body Lining. (To be Made as a Separate Waist or Attached to a Skirt as a One-Piece Dress.)

IMPORTANT NOTICE: For explanation of Outlet and Seam Allowances, and Diagram of Pattern Pieces, See Other Side.

BEFORE CUTTING, compare pattern pieces with diagram on back of envelope, and be SURE each pattern piece corresponds with its illustration.

PUBLISHED BY THE BUTTERICK PUBLISHING CO., NEW YORK, LONDON, PARIS.

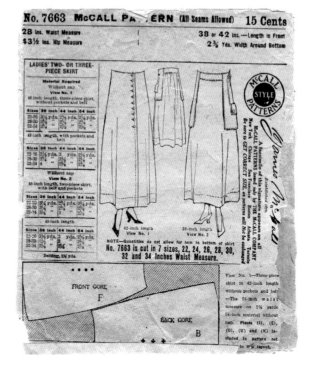

No. **7663** McCALL PATTERN (All Seams Allowed)   **15** Cents

28 ins. Waist Measure   38 or 42 ins.—Length in Front
43½ ins. Hip Measure   2⅜ Yds. Width Around Bottom

LADIES' TWO- OR THREE-PIECE SKIRT

McCALL STYLE PATTERNS

NOTE—Quantities do not allow for hem in bottom of skirt No. 7663 is cut in 7 sizes, 22, 24, 26, 28, 30, 32 and 34 Inches Waist Measure.

FRONT GORE F

BACK GORE B

One
major
influence:

**The 1925
Exposition
of Modern
Industrial and
Decorative Art**
(the birth of Art Deco)

CHAPTER TWO
1920-1929

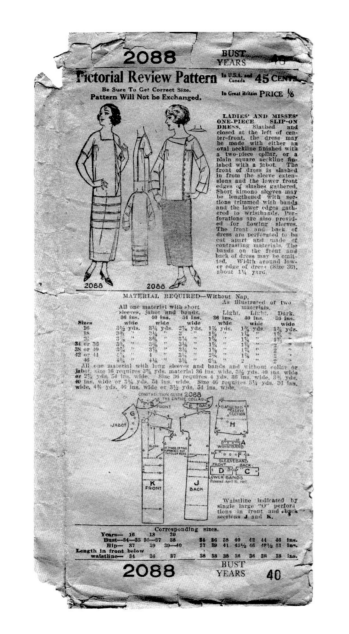

An early 1920s retro pattern.

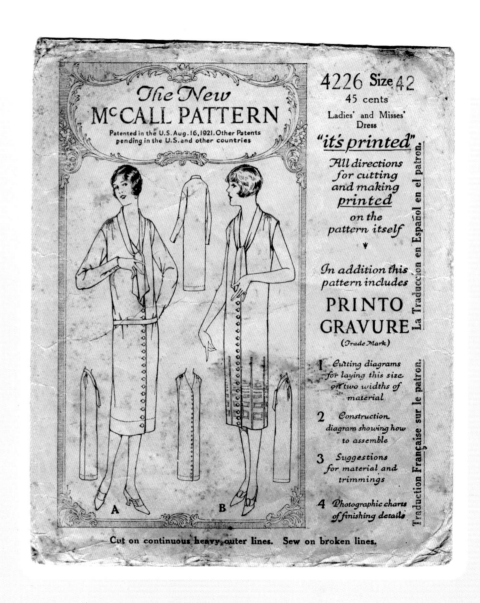

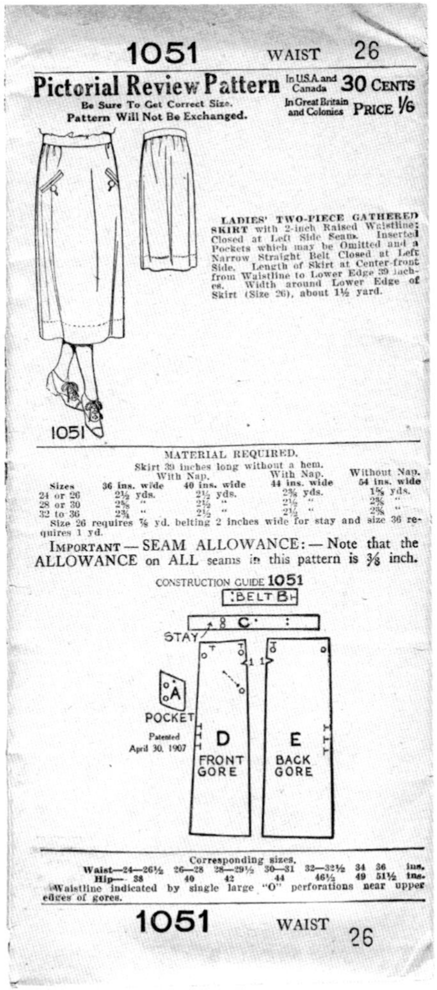

1051 WAIST 26

Pictorial Review Pattern In U.S.A. and Canada 30 CENTS In Great Britain and Colonies PRICE 1/6

Be Sure To Get Correct Size. Pattern Will Not Be Exchanged.

LADIES' TWO-PIECE GATHERED SKIRT with 2-inch Raised Waistline; Closed at Left Side Seam. Inserted Pockets which may be Omitted and a Narrow Straight Belt Closed at Left Side. Length of Skirt at Center-front from Waistline to Lower Edge 39 inches. Width around Lower Edge of Skirt (Size 26), about 1½ yard.

1051

MATERIAL REQUIRED.

Skirt 39 inches long without a hem.

Sizes	With Nap. 36 ins. wide	40 ins. wide	With Nap. 44 ins. wide	Without Nap. 54 ins. wide
24 or 26	2½ yds.	2½ yds.	2⅜ yds.	1⅝ yds.
28 or 30	2⅝ "	2½ "	2½ "	2⅜ "
32 to 36	2¾ "	2½ "	2½ "	2⅜ "

Size 26 requires ⅞ yd. belting 2 inches wide for stay and size 36 requires 1 yd.

IMPORTANT — SEAM ALLOWANCE: — Note that the ALLOWANCE on ALL seams in this pattern is ⅜ inch.

CONSTRUCTION GUIDE 1051

BELT B
C
STAY
A
POCKET
Patented April 30, 1907
D
FRONT GORE
E
BACK GORE

Corresponding sizes.

Waist—	24—26½	26—28	28—29½	30—31	32—32½	34	36 ins.
Hip—	38	40	42	44	46½	49	51½ ins.

Waistline indicated by single large "O" perforations near upper edges of gores.

1051 WAIST 26

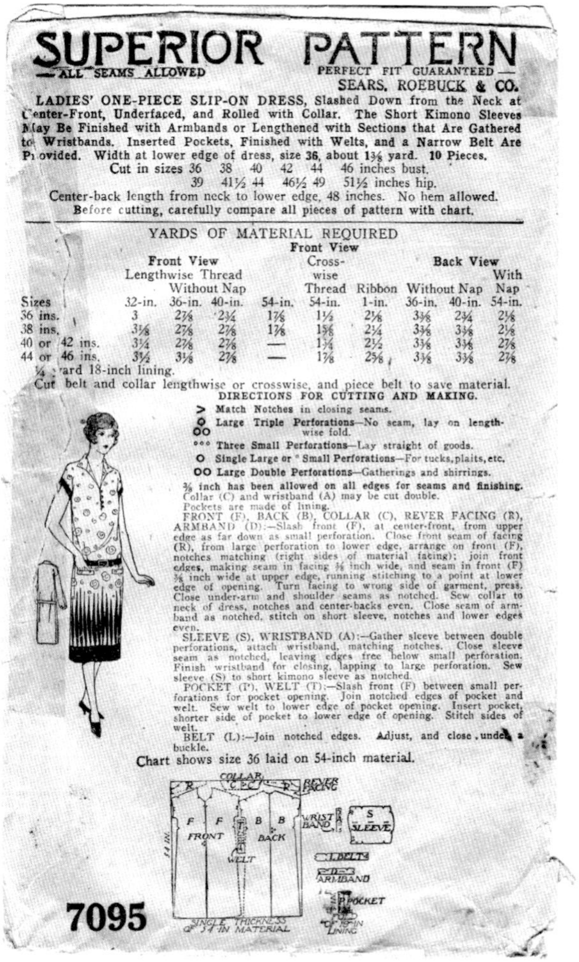

SUPERIOR PATTERN

—ALL SEAMS ALLOWED PERFECT FIT GUARANTEED — SEARS, ROEBUCK & CO.

LADIES' ONE-PIECE SLIP-ON DRESS, Slashed Down from the Neck at Center-Front, Underfaced, and Rolled with Collar. The Short Kimono Sleeves May Be Finished with Armbands or Lengthened with Sections that Are Gathered to Wristbands. Inserted Pockets, Finished with Welts, and a Narrow Belt Are Provided. Width at lower edge of dress, size 36, about 1⅜ yard. 10 Pieces.

Cut in sizes 36 38 40 42 44 46 inches bust.
39 41½ 44 46½ 49 51½ inches hip.

Center-back length from neck to lower edge, 48 inches. No hem allowed.
Before cutting, carefully compare all pieces of pattern with chart.

YARDS OF MATERIAL REQUIRED

Sizes	Front View Lengthwise Thread Without Nap 32-in.	36-in.	40-in.	54-in.	Front View Cross-wise Thread 54-in.	Ribbon 1-in.	Back View Without Nap 36-in.	40-in.	With Nap 54-in.
36 ins.	3	2⅞	2¾	1⅞	1½	2⅛	3⅜	2¾	2⅛
38 ins.	3⅛	2⅞	2⅞	1⅞	1⅝	2¼	3⅜	3⅛	2⅛
40 or 42 ins.	3¼	2⅞	2⅞	—	1¾	2½	3⅜	3⅛	2⅞
44 or 46 ins.	3½	3⅛	2⅞	—	1⅞	2⅝	3⅜	3⅜	2⅞

¼ yard 18-inch lining.

Cut belt and collar lengthwise or crosswise, and piece belt to save material.

DIRECTIONS FOR CUTTING AND MAKING.

> Match Notches in closing seams.
Large Triple Perforations—No seam, lay on lengthwise fold.
Three Small Perforations—Lay straight of goods.
Single Large or ° Small Perforations—For tucks, plaits, etc.
Large Double Perforations—Gatherings and shirrings.

⅜ inch has been allowed on all edges for seams and finishing.
Collar (C) and wristband (A) may be cut double.
Pockets are made of lining.

FRONT (F), BACK (B), COLLAR (C), REVER FACING (R), ARMBAND (D):—Slash front (F), at center-front, from upper edge as far down as small perforation. Close front seam of facing (R), from large perforation to lower edge, arrange on front (F), notches matching (right sides of material facing); join front edges, making seam in facing ⅜ inch wide, and seam in front (F) ⅜ inch wide at upper edge, running stitching to a point at lower edge of opening. Turn facing to wrong side of garment, press. Close under-arm and shoulder seams as notched. Sew collar to neck of dress, notches and center-backs even. Close seam of armband as notched, stitch on short sleeve, notches and lower edges even.

SLEEVE (S), WRISTBAND (A):—Gather sleeve between double perforations, attach wristband, matching notches. Close sleeve seam as notched, leaving edges free below small perforation. Finish wristband for closing, lapping to large perforation. Sew sleeve (S) to short kimono sleeve as notched.

POCKET (P), WELT (T):—Slash front (F) between small perforations for pocket opening. Join notched edges of pocket and welt. Sew welt to lower edge of pocket opening. Insert pocket, shorter side of pocket to lower edge of opening. Stitch sides of welt.

BELT (L):—Join notched edges. Adjust, and close under a buckle.

Chart shows size 36 laid on 54-inch material.

7095

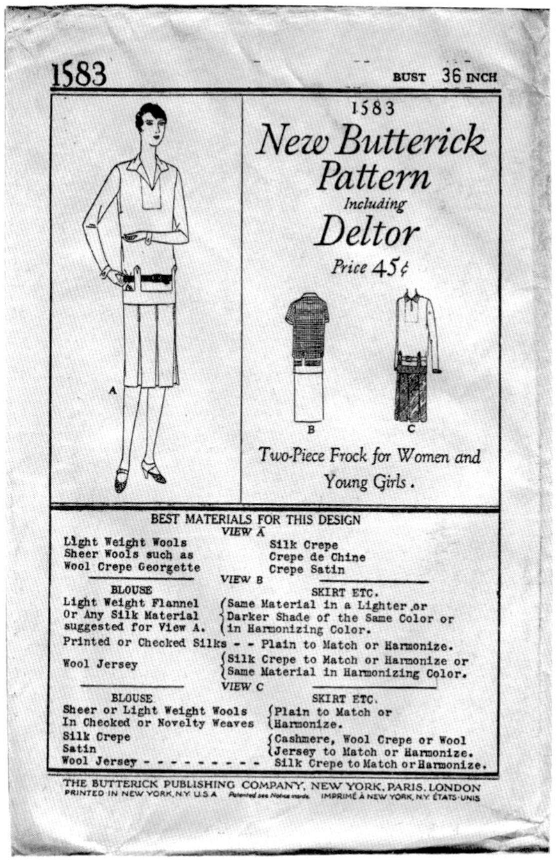

1583 BUST 36 INCH

1583

New Butterick Pattern Including Deltor

Price 45¢

A B C

Two-Piece Frock for Women and Young Girls.

BEST MATERIALS FOR THIS DESIGN

VIEW A

Light Weight Wools
Sheer Wools such as
Wool Crepe Georgette

Silk Crepe
Crepe de Chine
Crepe Satin

VIEW B

BLOUSE	SKIRT ETC.
Light Weight Flannel Or Any Silk Material suggested for View A.	Same Material in a Lighter or Darker Shade of the Same Color or in Harmonizing Color.
Printed or Checked Silks	Plain to Match or Harmonize.
Wool Jersey	Silk Crepe to Match or Harmonize or Same Material in Harmonizing Color.

VIEW C

BLOUSE	SKIRT ETC.
Sheer or Light Weight Wools In Checked or Novelty Weaves	Plain to Match or Harmonize.
Silk Crepe Satin	Cashmere, Wool Crepe or Wool Jersey to Match or Harmonize.
Wool Jersey	Silk Crepe to Match or Harmonize.

THE BUTTERICK PUBLISHING COMPANY, NEW YORK, PARIS, LONDON
PRINTED IN NEW YORK, N.Y. U.S.A. Patented see Notice inside. IMPRIMÉ À NEW YORK, N.Y. ÉTATS-UNIS

McCall's was one of the first to use
color printing in their illustrations.

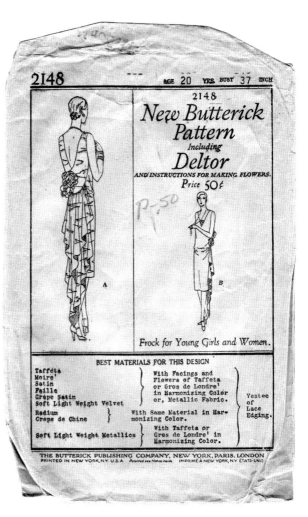

A transitional style, between the 1920s flapper and the 1930s.

Two
major
influences:

- The Depression
- Hollywood

CHAPTER THREE

1930-1939

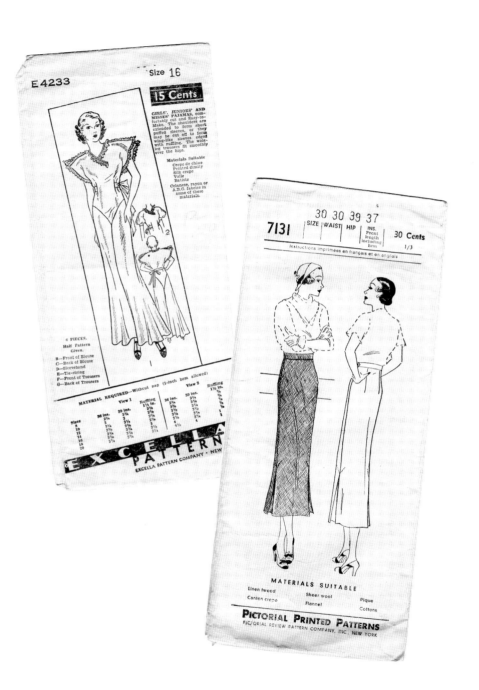

E 4233   Size 16

15 Cents

GIRLS', JUNIORS' AND MISSES' PAJAMAS, comfortably cut and Easy-to-Make. The shoulders are extended to form short puffed sleeves, or they may be cut off to form wing-like sleeves edged with ruffling. The wide-leg trousers fit smoothly over the hips.

Materials Suitable
Crepe de chine
Printed dimity
Silk crepe
Voile
Batiste
Celanese, rayon or A.B.C. fabrics in some of these materials.

6 PIECES.
Half Pattern Given.
B—Front of Blouse
C—Back of Blouse
D—Sleeveband
E—Tie-string
F—Front of Trousers
G—Back of Trousers

MATERIAL REQUIRED—Without nap (1-inch hem allowed)

EXCELLA PATTERN
EXCELLA PATTERN COMPANY · NEW

7131   SIZE 30 WAIST 30 HIP 39 INS. 37   30 Cents
Front length including hem   1/3

Instructions imprimées en français et en anglais

MATERIALS SUITABLE
Linen tweed   Sheer wool
Canton crepe   Flannel   Pique
                                      Cottons

PICTORIAL PRINTED PATTERNS
PICTORIAL REVIEW PATTERN COMPANY, INC., NEW YORK

1182   Size 14

PRICE
15c

FIGURE 1   FIGURE 2   FIGURE 3

SIMPLICITY PATTERN
WITH THE SIMPLICITY PRIMER

1346

Bust 34   Size 16

Hip 37"

Hip measured 7" below normal waistline

SEAM ALLOWANCE ⅜" ON ALL EDGES

10 Cents

WOMEN'S, MISSES' and JUNIORS' BLOUSE. This is a flattering well-tailored design provided with a choice of sleeves, the long bishop style and the short puff affairs. The Peter Pan collar gives a jaunty air to this simple blouse and the opening at the throat may be neatly linked together with two buttons. The tie-belt is arranged in three-quarter style about the waist. Perforations provide for a shorter length.

1

2

ADVANCE PATTERNS
NEW YORK   PARIS   LONDON

1461

Bust 34   Size 16

Hip 37"

Hip measured 7" below normal waistline.

SEAM ALLOWANCE ⅜" ON ALL EDGES

10 Cents

WOMEN'S, MISSES' and JUNIORS' TWO-PIECE PAJAMA. This two-piece design is attractively styled for the beginner with special step-by-step illustrated instructions. The kimona sleeves are cut in one with the overblouse and may be shirred to a narrow sleeveband or cut through along the line of perforations. Observe the choice of a high, round or V-shape neckline. Length of trousers at side seam, size 16, 42 inches with a 1-inch hem; width of each leg about ⅞ yard.

2

1

Printed in U.S.A.

ADVANCE PATTERNS
NEW YORK   PARIS   LONDON

18

P-50

Simplicity Pattern 1402 Size 18
NEW YORK   PARIS   LONDON

Price 15¢ ... 9d

NRA
WE DO OUR PART

You are always in style when you dress with "SIMPLICITY"

Circa 1933, very long legs and long skirts were "the look." Full color in Simplicity illustration.

Price 15¢...9d **Simplicity Pattern** 1553 Bust 36 Hip 39 **36**

LONDON · PARIS · NEW YORK

MADE IN U. S. A.
NRA

You are always in style when you dress with "SIMPLICITY"

Price 15¢...9d **Simplicity Pattern** 1572 Size 16 Bust 34 **16**

LONDON · PARIS · NEW YORK

...le when yo... ...e SIMPLICITY

Simplicity Pattern 1871 NEW YORK PARIS LONDON

Bust 36 Hip 39

36

Price 15¢...9d   MADE IN U.S.A.

1   2

5165   Size 18

25c

1   3

Excella

THE HIGH STYLE–LOW PRICED PATTERN

with the new

EXCELLAGRAF FOR SIMPLER SEWING

Simplicity Pattern 2095 NEW YORK PARIS LONDON

Bust 36 Hip 39

36

Price 15¢...9d   MADE IN U.S.A.

1   2

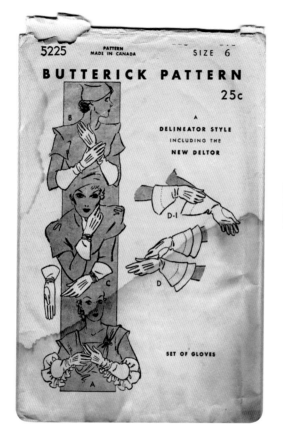

5225 PATTERN MADE IN CANADA SIZE 6

BUTTERICK PATTERN
25c

A
DELINEATOR STYLE
INCLUDING THE
NEW DELTOR

D-I

D

SET OF GLOVES

5974	14	32	35	47	35 Cents
	SIZE	BUST	HIP	INS. Back length	1/-

Instructions imprimées en français et en anglais

1 2

MATERIALS SUITABLE

Crepe de chine   Flat crepe   Satin

Radium silk   Ninon   Flat crepe

View 1—Lace edging for trim.

Celanese, rayon or Bemberg in some of the above materials.

PICTORIAL PRINTED PATTERNS
THE PICTORIAL REVIEW COMPANY, NEW YORK

995B   Size 16

3.00

duBarry
PATTERNS

10c EACH   6d IN THE BRITISH ISLES

SMART
PATTERNS
FOR
SMART
WOMEN

MADE IN U. S. A.

NRA

With ILLUSTRATED INSTRUCTIONS for CUTTING and SEWING

NO. 7202   SIZE 18
                                  36 BUST 39 HIP

VOGUE
PATTERN

PRICE 50c

P-150

C

"EASY-TO-MAKE"
ONE-PIECE FROCK CUT IN
SIZES . . 12—14—16—18—20—40—42

B
© Vogue
A

42

42

Bust 42
Hip 45

2398

Simplicity Pattern
NEW YORK
PARIS
LONDON

PRICE 25c ...1/-

MADE IN U.S.A.

Meier & Frank Co.
DOWNSTAIRS STORE

1   2

7258 SIZE 16 34 BUST

45c

Junior Miss Frock with Four-Gored Skirt Attached at Natural Waistline.

COMPANION ~ BUTTERICK
PATTERN INCLUDING THE DELTOR

7296 SIZE 16 34 BUST

45c

Junior Miss Bolero Jacket Frock. Attached Six-Gored Flared Skirt. Kimono Sleeve. Sun-Back or Higher Neck. Bolero Jacket.

COMPANION ~ BUTTERICK
PATTERN INCLUDING THE DELTOR

NO. 7601　　　　　　　SIZE 16
　　　　　　　　　34 BUST 37 HIP

VOGUE PATTERN

PRICE 50c

ONE-PIECE FROCK CUT IN
SIZES . . . . 12—14—16—18—20

"EASY-TO-MAKE"

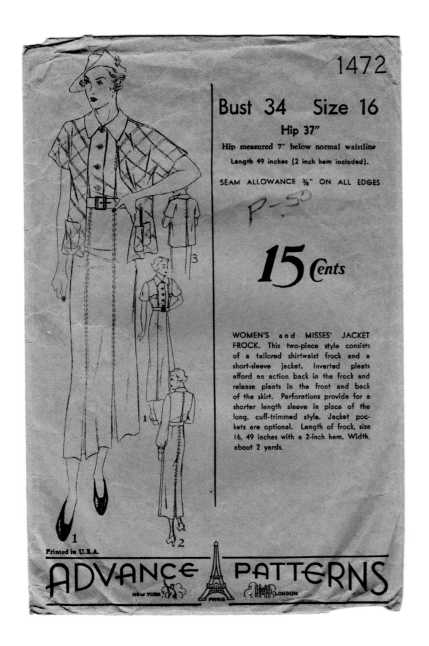

1472

Bust 34   Size 16

Hip 37"

Hip measured 7" below normal waistline

Length 49 inches (2 inch hem included).

SEAM ALLOWANCE ⅜" ON ALL EDGES

P-50

15 Cents

WOMEN'S and MISSES' JACKET FROCK. This two-piece style consists of a tailored shirtwaist frock and a short-sleeve jacket. Inverted pleats afford an action back in the frock and release pleats in the front and back of the skirt. Perforations provide for a shorter length sleeve in place of the long, cuff-trimmed style. Jacket pockets are optional. Length of frock, size 16, 49 inches with a 2-inch hem. Width, about 2 yards.

Printed in U.S.A.

ADVANCE PATTERNS

NEW YORK   PARIS   LONDON

NO. 6975

SIZE 16
34 BUST 37 HIP

VOGUE PATTERN

PRICE 50c

⑨ PT-1-12
$2.00 ND

ONE-PIECE FROCK CUT IN
SIZES . . . 12—14—16—18—20—40

© Vogue

A rare New York pattern, circa 1934.

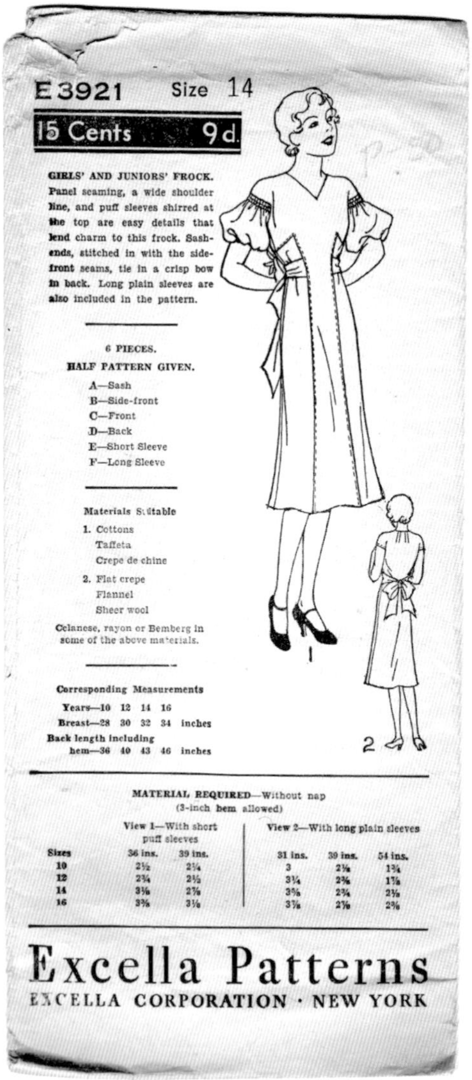
E3921 Size 14
15 Cents 9d.
GIRLS' AND JUNIORS' FROCK. Panel seaming, a wide shoulder line, and puff sleeves shirred at the top are easy details that lend charm to this frock. Sash-ends, stitched in with the side-front seams, tie in a crisp bow in back. Long plain sleeves are also included in the pattern.
6 PIECES.
HALF PATTERN GIVEN.
A—Sash
B—Side-front
C—Front
D—Back
E—Short Sleeve
F—Long Sleeve
Materials Suitable
1. Cottons
Taffeta
Crepe de chine
2. Flat crepe
Flannel
Sheer wool
Celanese, rayon or Bemberg in some of the above materials.
Corresponding Measurements
Years—10 12 14 16
Breast—28 30 32 34 inches
Back length including hem—36 40 43 46 inches
1
2
MATERIAL REQUIRED—Without nap
(3-inch hem allowed)
View 1—With short puff sleeves
View 2—With long plain sleeves
Sizes 36 ins. 39 ins. 31 ins. 39 ins. 54 ins.
10 2½ 2¼ 3 2⅛ 1¾
12 2¾ 2½ 3¼ 2⅜ 1⅞
14 3⅛ 2⅞ 3⅝ 2¾ 2⅛
16 3⅜ 3⅛ 3⅞ 2⅞ 2⅜
Excella Patterns
EXCELLA CORPORATION · NEW YORK

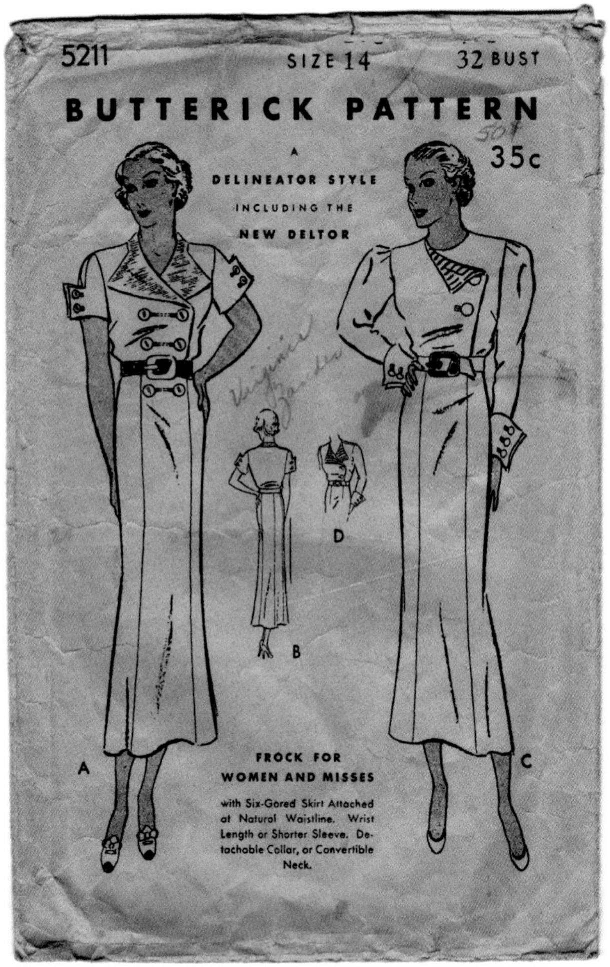
5211 SIZE 14 32 BUST
BUTTERICK PATTERN
35c
A
DELINEATOR STYLE
INCLUDING THE
NEW DELTOR
A B C D
FROCK FOR WOMEN AND MISSES
with Six-Gored Skirt Attached at Natural Waistline. Wrist Length or Shorter Sleeve. Detachable Collar, or Convertible Neck.

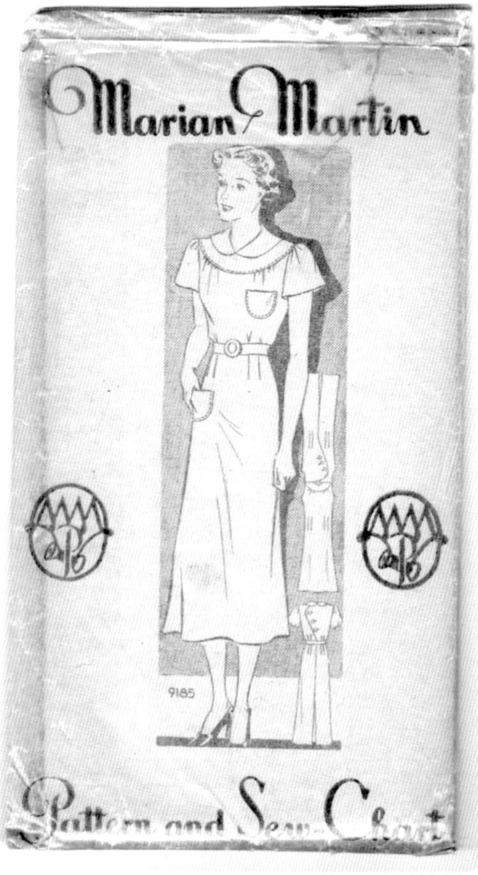
Marian Martin
9185
Pattern and Sew-Chart

5273 SIZE **14** **32** BUST

50¢

BUTTERICK PATTERN

A
DELINEATOR STYLE
INCLUDING THE
NEW DELTOR

50c

A

B

D

C

**SUIT FOR
WOMEN AND MISSES**

Jacket with Collar in Either of
Two Styles. Four-Piece Bias
or Straight Cut Skirt. (For
Diagonal Fabrics with Both
Sides Alike.)

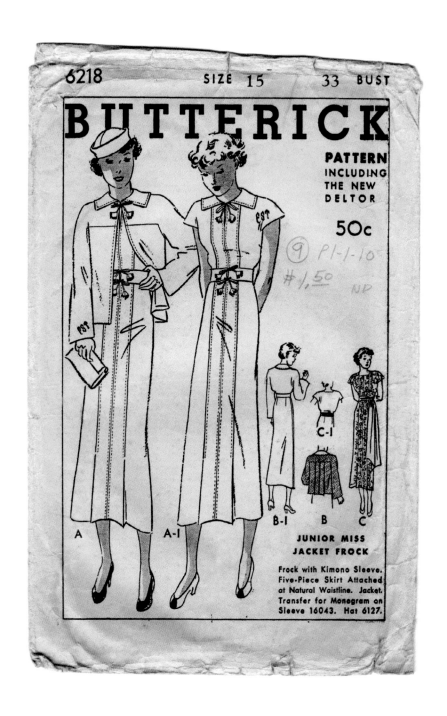

6218 SIZE **15** **33** BUST

BUTTERICK

PATTERN
INCLUDING
THE NEW
DELTOR

50c

A   A-1   B-1   B   C
C-1

**JUNIOR MISS
JACKET FROCK**

Frock with Kimono Sleeve.
Five-Piece Skirt Attached
at Natural Waistline. Jacket.
Transfer for Monogram on
Sleeve 16043. Hat 6127.

1930-1939

SIZE 18 36 BUST
39 HIP 1110

ANITA LOUISE
WARNER BROS.

A SEW-SIMPLE
DESIGN

THE
DE LUXE
15 CENT
PATTERN

HOLLYWOOD ★★★★ **PATTERN**

1791B
Size 18
Bust 36

10c
EACH
6d in the
British Isles
MADE IN U.S.A.

DuBarry
GUARANTEED
PATTERNS

WITH ILLUSTRATED INSTRUCTIONS for CUTTING and SEWING

1202 14 YEARS

HOLLYWOOD PATTERN

★ THE
★ DE LUXE
★ 15 CENT
★ PATTERN

A SEW-SIMPLE DESIGN

Ladies' and Misses' Peasant Apron

Choose strong vibrant colors for this apron to bring out its true peasant character—and not only for the cross-stitch but for the contrasting bands at top and bottom. You can make it as gay as you like—the gayer it is the more you'll enjoy it.

McCALL
PRINTED PATTERN with TRANSFER
406 ONE SIZE
30c
YELLOW OR BLUE
BLUE

22-913d
c.1936
$1.00

Simplicity Pattern
PARIS
LONDON   NEW YORK
2439
414 1
Bust 36
Hip 39
36
15c 9d
MADE IN U.S.A.

By 1936, skirts were a little shorter.

NO. 7891—50c

VOGUE PATTERN

SIZE 12
30 BUST 33 HIP

25¢

B

A

© Vogue

15c 1804

Advance

BUST 42

Hip 45"

Finished Length 49"

Width about 2¼ yds.

4.00

Including Improved
Step-by-Step
Dressmaking GUIDE

2

1

PRINTED IN U.S.A.

ADVANCE PATTERNS
NEW YORK   PARIS   LONDON

Light Weight Wools – – – Velveteen or Same Fabric In Contrast

6982   SIZE 14   32 BREAST

25c

E

B   Ci   C   A   D

Juniors' and Girls' Frock.
Four-Piece Skirt Attached
to Body. Two Styles of
Sleeves. Peplum Optional.
Purchased Flowers.

BUTTERICK
PATTERN INCLUDING THE DELTOR

VOGUE

EXCLUSIVE DESIGN
CREATED BY VOGUE

⑨ PI-1-14
$2.00 ND

NO. 498

COUTURIER PATTERN

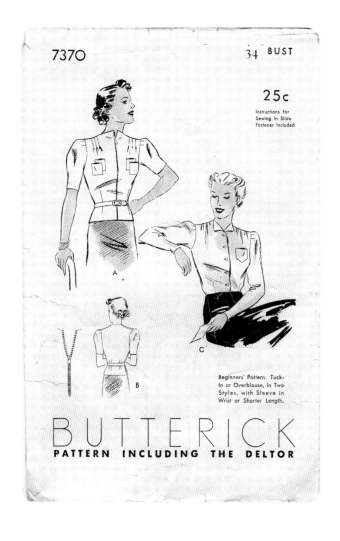

7370   34 BUST

25c

Instructions for
Sewing in Slide
Fastener Included

A

B   C

Beginners' Pattern. Tuck-
In or Overblouse, in Two
Styles, with Sleeve in
Wrist or Shorter Length.

BUTTERICK
PATTERN INCLUDING THE DELTOR

A Versatile **COAT** for Dressy or Tailored Frocks

15¢ each

ADVANCE 1656. Frock. 15 Cents. Sizes 14 to 20 years; 34 to 44 bust. Size 16 requires 3⅛ yards 54-inch checked wool, ¼ yard 39-inch contrast for scarf.

ADVANCE 1654. Frock. 15 Cents. Sizes 12 to 20 years; 34 to 38 bust. Size 16 requires 3½ yards 39-inch crepe. An easy afternoon frock to make and to wear.

ADVANCE 1651. Coat. 15 Cents. Sizes 14 to 20 years; 34 to 40 bust. Size 16—3½ yards 54-inch duvetyn, 2¾ yards 39-inch lining, 1⅜ yards fur banding.

1651   1656   1654

ADVANCE PATTERNS

December, 1936   Page 3

DISTINCTION Attained Through Tucks and Shirring

15¢ each

ADVANCE 1667. Frock. 15 Cents. Sizes 34 to 46 bust. Size 16 requires 3¾ yards 39-inch velvet. Rows of shirring on either shoulder introduce soft bodice fullness.

ADVANCE 1657. Frock. 15 Cents. Sizes 14 to 20 years; 34 to 40 bust. Size 16 requires 3½ yards 39-inch silk. A grand accessory frock with a choice of sleeves.

ADVANCE 1655. Two-piece Frock. 15 Cents. Sizes 12 to 20 years; 34 to 38 bust. Size 16 requires 2⅝ yards 54-inch thin wool, ½ yard 39-inch contrast.

1667   1657   1655

ARE QUALITY PATTERNS

December, 1936   Page 7

Velvets and satins for **FORMAL** afternoons and evenings

15¢ each

ADVANCE 1668. Evening Coat. 15 Cents. Sizes 14 to 20 years; 34 to 38 bust. Size 16—7⅞ yards 39-inch velvet, 4¼ yards 39-inch lining, 6 yards 36-inch interlining.

ADVANCE 1647. Frock. 15 Cents. Sizes 12 to 20 years; 34 to 40 bust. Size 16 requires 4⅞ yards 39-inch satin. A slim princess model with a choice of skirt lengths.

ADVANCE 1643. Frock. 15 Cents. Sizes 14 to 20 years; 34 to 38 bust. Size 16 requires 3½ yards 39-inch crepe. Fashionable back fullness for afternoons.

1668   1647   1643

ARE QUALITY PATTERNS

Score in Chic With These Winning **ADVANCE**
Designs Priced for Budget Wardrobes

15¢ — each

ADVANCE 1638. Frock. 15 Cents. Sizes 14 to 20 years; 34 to 38 bust. Size 16 requires 3⅞ yards 39-inch crepe. The popular swing skirt in a form-fitting frock with tie neckline for velvet or satin.

ADVANCE 1644. Frock. 15 Cents. Sizes 14 to 20 years; 34 to 38 bust. Size 16 requires 2⅝ yards 54-inch broadcloth, ½ yard 39-inch contrast for facing and belt. The frock of the moment with shoulder darts.

ADVANCE 1633. Frock. 15 Cents. Sizes 14 to 20 years; 34 to 38 bust. Size 16 requires 3 yards 39-inch candlewick crepe, 1½ yards 2-inch ribbon for scarf. Pick one of the new tufted fabrics for this distinctive design.

ADVANCE 1646. Frock. 15 Cents. Sizes 14 to 20 years; 34 to 42 bust. Size 16 requires 3⅜ yards 39-inch challis print, ⅜ yard 36-inch pique. The pert collar accents the tailored quality of this easily made frock.

ADVANCE 1632. Frock. 15 Cents. Sizes 12 to 20 years; 34 to 38 bust. Size 16 requires 2¾ yards 54-inch thin wool. Buttoned down the front for a tailored accent to an otherwise soft semi-princess silhouette.

ADVANCE 1635. Coat. 15 Cents. Sizes 14 to 20 years; 34 to 40 bust. Size 16 requires 4¼ yards 54-inch duvetyn, 3¾ yards 39-inch lining, 4⅜ yards 36-inch interlining, ½ yard 48-inch fur cloth. The princess coat.

ADVANCE 1642. Frock. Sizes 14 to 20 years; 3... Size 16 requires 3⅜ y... velvet, ½ yard 39-inch... scarf. Seamed for a... silhouette with buil... and extended should...

1644   1633   1646   1638   1632   1635   1642

• ✂ • A D V A N C E   P A T T E R N S   A R E   Q U A L I T Y   P A T T E...

Hollywood Pattern

1160   SIZE 14 32 BUST 35 HIP

CLAUDETTE COLBERT A PARAMOUNT STAR

★ THE
★ DE LUXE
★ 15 CENT
★ PATTERN

© THE H. P. CO.

A recurring detail — see *Chapter 2* Cosmopolitan pattern.

My mother used this Hollywood pattern to make me a dress in the 1980s.

SILHOUETTE

is The News of the Month.

By Barbara Godfrey,

With Paris introducing fashions to conform with the new sculptured silhouette featured at the Paris exposition one will find it necessary to select the right foundation garment before considering the new designs. The figure is glorified by draping the curves of the bust and hip and this in effect slenderizes the waist and returns the feminine form to its original natural lines. Regardless of size, any silhouette will be enhanced by the style details of the new fashions.

Advance No. 1898 will please the eye immediately with its shirred draping from the yoke and slightly broadened shoulders. The repeated yoke detail at the waistline appears to emphasize the smallness of the mid-section. In wool or crepe No. 1898 is a happy choice.

A set of two blouses is Advance No. 1901 — one for your tailored moods and the other for your more dressy occasions. This plan for changes with your winter suit is a "must" this year.

Advance No. 1903 is so versatile a whole wardrobe could be planned from this one pattern. The skirt and blouse that is so carefully worked out in detail may be made of one material in a matelasse, crepe or printed silk, which would result in a charming frock or of contrasting materials for a blouse and skirt effect. Then it can be made as a lovely suit with its princess lines and fur-trimmed lower edge. Buttoned down the front with its youthful collar you will find it one of the smartest outfits for any occasion. The coat may also be made full length and worn separately over any frock.

Brides are always in season but the pre-holiday bride demands much attention. The happy miss gowned in Advance No. 1905 is sure to be the st===s of the season. This simply cut dress with its high molded bust line and flattering lace collar and vestee made in satin which the design will flatter she will thrill every guest and surely the Groom.

If you are one that aims to finish a frock quickly try Advance No. 1912. This consists of a front and back darted at the waistline with a collar, belt and sleeves. One of those frocks can be started and finished in a few hours before a date, and is so smart in either light weight woolens or crepes.

The draped bodice and skirt front of Advance No. 1902 is truly distinctive for satin or crepe with its tiny rolled collar and slim waistline.

A broadened shoulder need not be darted or gathered when cleverly cut as Advance No. 1909 with its raglan sleeve. A simple frock trimmed with an interesting belt.

Another school-frock for the younger member is always welcome. For the new corduroy look in Advance No. 1911. Girlish to the last degree is this two-piece style with its patch pockets and small collar.

Barbara Godfrey, Advance Pattern Co.
635 Greenwich Street, New York, N. Y.

1904

1903

November, 1937

MOLDED WAISTLINE
OR BOXY JACKET
SUIT AND ENSEMBLE

ADVANCE 1903. Ensemble. Price 35 Cents. Sizes 14 to 20 years: 32 to 38 bust. Size 16 requires 3¾ yards 54-inch wool. 1⅞ yards 39-inch contrast for blouse. 2¼ yards 39-inch lining. 2½ yards fur banding.

ADVANCE 1904. Suit. Price 25 Cents. Sizes 14 to 20 years: 32 to 38 bust. Size 16 requires 2⅞ yards 54-inch fur cloth, 2½ yards 39-inch lining, 1⅜ yards 54-inch wool for skirt. Equally smart in all wool.

1909   1914   1913   1914   1913

SCULPTURED SILHOUETTES

Description of designs on front cover

ADVANCE 1914. Frock. Price 15 Cents. Sizes 14 to 20 years: 32 to 38 bust. Size 16 requires 2¼ yards 54-inch wool, ⅜ yard 39-inch contrast. A simple tailored dress with diagonal closing.

ADVANCE 1912. Frock. Price 15 Cents. Sizes 12 to 20 years: 30 to 40 bust. Size 16 requires 3¾ yards 39-inch satin ¼ yard 39-inch contrast. A one piece frock with zipper closing and contrasting collar.

ADVANCE 1909. Frock. Price 15 Cents. Sizes 14 to 20 years: 32 to 38 bust. Size 16 requires 2½ yards 54-inch wool. ¼ yard 54-inch contrast for girdle. The new raglan sleeve with broadened shoulders and patch pockets.

ADVANCE 1913. Frock. Price 15 Cents. Sizes 14 to 20 years: 30 to 40 bust. Size 16 requires 3¾ yards 39-inch satin, ¼ yard 39-inch crepe contrast. Buttoned from a diagonal line on the bodice straight down the front.

ADVANCE 1913. Frock. Price 15 Cents. Sizes 14 to 20 years: 30 to 40 bust. Size 16 requires 3¾ yards 39-inch crepe, ¼ yard 39-inch contrast. A princess frock with belted waistline and contrasting V shape collar.

Advance Fashions

SCULPTURED SILHOUETTES   AND
FOR TAILORED AND   AFTER

1898

1902   1900

ADVANCE 1898. Frock. Price 15 Cents. Sizes 12 to 20 years: 30 to 38 bust. Size 16 requires 2½ yards 54-inch thin wool, ½ yard 39-inch contrast. Shirred to a front panel to give the slim waistline effect.

Advance Fash

1930-1939

e 15
30 to
ailed
r the
ollar.

e 15
32 to
ards
e six
n sil-
ened

e 15
32 to
ards
con-
tiny
aist-

e 25
S116
satin,
outh-
e sil-
bust.

e 15
30 to
ards
bbon,
ers.

r, 1937

1907

1902 1900 1898 1907 1896 1906

5

A BRIDE'S TROUSSEAU

ADVANCE 1909. Frock. Price 15 Cents. Sizes 14 to 20 years; 32 to 38 bust. Size 16 requires 2⅜ yards 54-inch plaid. A youthful tailored frock for Fall and Winter. Frock may also be made with long sleeves.

ADVANCE 1905. Frock. Price 25 Cents. Sizes 14 to 20 years; 32 to 38 bust. Size 16 requires 6¼ yards 39-inch satin, ½ yard 36-inch lace. A gown of sweet simplicity with a flattering lace collar for the bride.

ADVANCE 1908. Frock. Price 25 Cents. Sizes 34 to 42 bust. Size 34 requires 5⅛ yards 39-inch crepe, 1¾ yards 36-inch lace for blouse. A formal dinner frock for the bride's mother. Jacket is removable.

ADVANCE 1903. Ensemble. Price 35 Cents. Sizes 14 to 20 years; 32 to 38 bust. Size 16, skirt and blouse only requires 1⅛ yards 54-inch light weight woolen, 1¾ yards 39-inch embroidered novelty cloth for blouse.

ADVANCE 1904. Suit. Price 25 Cents. Sizes 14 to 20 years; 32 to 38 bust. Size 16 requires 3⅜ yards 54-inch wool, 3⅛ yards 39-inch lining. A two-piece suit with a three-quarter length boxy jacket.

Advance Fashions

1905

1903

1909

1908

1904

6

SIMPLE LINES FOR
WOOL AND CREPE

ADVANCE **1913.** Frock. Price 15 Cents. Sizes 12 to 20 years; 30 to 40 bust. Size 16 requires 3¼ yards 39-inch material. A smart frock with zipper front. May also be made with long sleeves and contrasting collar.

ADVANCE **1911.** Two piece Frock. Price 15 Cents. Sizes 12 to 20 years; 30 to 40 bust. Size 16 requires 2¼ yards 54-inch plaid. A two-piece frock easily made for the school miss, that can be tucked in or worn outside the skirt.

ADVANCE **1897.** Frock. Price 15 Cents. Sizes 12 to 20 years; 30 to 38 bust. Size 16 requires 2⅝ yards 54-inch wool, ⅞ yard ribbon to trim. Broken princess lines with a fly-front closing and tiny revers.

ADVANCE **1899.** Frock. Price 15 Cents. Sizes 12 to 20 years; 30 to 40 bust. Size 16 requires 3⅜ yards 36-inch rayon. Equally smart in a printed silk, wool or satin. Emphasizing the slender waistline with a corded belt.

ADVANCE **1915.** Frock. Price 15 Cents. Sizes 14 to 20 years; 32 to 42 bust. Size 16 requires 2¾ yards 54-inch wool, ⅞ yard 39-inch contrast, 1⅞ yards ruffling. A flattering tailored frock with youthful neckline.

November, 1937

7

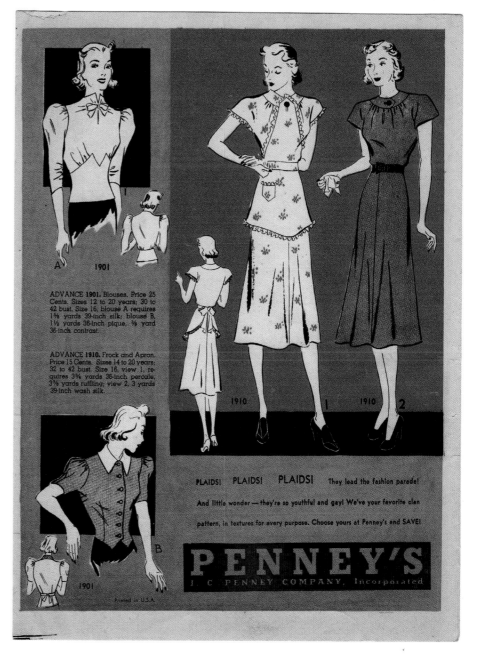

ADVANCE **1901.** Blouses. Price 25 Cents. Sizes 12 to 20 years; 30 to 42 bust. Size 16; blouse A requires 1⅝ yards 39-inch silk; blouse B, 1½ yards 36-inch pique, ⅜ yard 36-inch contrast.

ADVANCE **1910.** Frock and Apron. Price 15 Cents. Sizes 14 to 20 years; 32 to 42 bust. Size 16, view 1, requires 3¼ yards 36-inch percale, 3⅞ yards ruffling; view 2, 3 yards 39-inch wash silk.

PLAIDS! PLAIDS! PLAIDS! They lead the fashion parade!

And little wonder — they're so youthful and gay! We've your favorite clan

pattern, in textures for every purpose. Choose yours at Penney's and SAVE!

PENNEY'S
J. C. PENNEY COMPANY, Incorporated

Printed in U.S.A.

785B

Bust 42
Hip 45

352

10c
EACH
6d in the
British Isles

MADE IN U.S.A.

DuBarry
GUARANTEED
PATTERNS

With ILLUSTRATED INSTRUCTIONS CUTTING and S

1832B
Size 14

15c
EACH

Made in Canada

DuBarry
GUARANTEED
PATTERNS

With ILLUSTRATED INSTRUCTIONS for CUTTING and

1662   12 YEARS

HOLLYWOOD ★★★PATTERN OF YOUTH

1

2

15c

SIMPLICITY

9360

60th ANNIVERSARY PATTERN
LE PATRON DU *60ème* ANNIVERSAIRE

60¢ U.S.
Canada $2.25
B

SIZE RR (14-20)

0 39363 05088

PATTERN/PATRON

Simplicity Pattern

NEW YORK

PARIS

LONDON

Size 18
Bust 36

3067

18

PRICE 15¢

MADE IN U.S.A.

Simplicity printed patterns were 10 cents more than perforated ones.

1813

15c 42 BUST 15 HIP

OLIVIA DE HAVILLAND STARRED IN "DODGE CITY", A WARNER BROS. PRODUCTION

Hollywood

PATTERN OF YOUTH

2

1

1

© THE H. P. CO.

McCall

PRINTED PATTERN

3544
SIZE 44
Ladies' & Misses' Dress 25c

A

B

A Butterick junior miss frock, circa 1937, still a black and white illustration.

House Coat Fashions

THAT ARE SWEEPING THE COUNTRY

$3.50

Femininely lovely, dramatically bright, casually practical. Arrayed stunningly against the screen of fashion are three more handsome, unusual House Coats for the new season.

STYLE D. "Thistledown." Cuddly warm **Embossed Velour** in an all-over pattern. Wrap-around style with revere neck-line. Warm and practical yet the newest note in chic. Colors: **Dusky Pink** or **Aqua**. Sizes 14, 16, 18 and 20, also sizes 42 and 44.

STYLE E. "Marie Antoinette." Dresden-like in its daintiness, glamorous in its full skirted sweep. Fast color fine **Broadcloth**, washes beautifully. Multi-colored as shown. Sizes 14, 16, 18 and 20.

STYLE F. "Prince Albert." Dramatic, cleverly manipulated satin striped **Rayon Taffeta**. Designed to make a prettier, slimmer You! Slide fastener closing. Color as shown only. Sizes 14, 16, 18 and 20.
State Style, Size and Color when Ordering.

Style D

Style E

Style F

America's Smartest HOUSE COATS $3.50

Style A

Style B

Style C

You'll Wear Them . Morning Noon and Night

If you like formality when lounging . . . if you want the flattery of long lines and gay colors . . . if you've fallen in love with nipped-in waists and voluminous skirts choose one of this collection of new Fall House Coats. Tailored or gracefully feminine, each garment is cut full in length with an amazing sweep to the skirt. Careful attention has been paid to such details as slide fasteners, buttons and seams.

STYLE A. "Starlight." Handsome rayon **Satin** with a cunning waistcoat quilted in a charming manner. Slide fastener closing. Colors: **Starlight Blue** and **Wine**. Sizes 14, 16, 18 and 20.

STYLE B. "Tahiti." Dramatic tropical flowers splashed across practical, washable **Seersucker**. Wrap around style with a flattering revere style neck-line. Multi-colored print. Sizes 14, 16, 18 and 20, also sizes 42 and 44.

STYLE C. "Beau Catcher." Print little rows of dainty flowers march down the full skirt and the slim waist of this charming, young looking model. Rows and rows of elastic shirring hug the waistline. Slide fastener and a so clever sleeve. Excellent rayon **Taffeta**. Colors: **Dubonnet** or **Royal Blue**. Sizes 14, 16, 18 and 20.

Slip into a House Coat when you jump out of bed — look dew-drop fresh at the breakfast table.

Your luncheon guests will admire your chic practicality as hostess and cook in a "swishy" House Coat.

Gay enough to make an occasion of your quiet evenings at home.

DuBarry
15¢
GUARANTEED
PATTERNS

2426B
Size 18
Bust 36

50¢

Copyright, 1939 Du Barry Patterns Ltd.

NO. 8991—35c

40 BUST 43 HIP

VOGUE
PATTERN

25¢

©Vogue

406   15¢   36 BUST 39 HIP

HOLLYWOOD PATTERNS

Simplicity Pattern   NEW YORK
PARIS   LONDON
2802   Size 14   Bust 32

22.76N
Tennis
Pattern 50¢

PRICE 15¢ ... 9d
MADE IN U.S.A.

2287B
Size 16
Bust 34

10c

EACH
6d in the
British Isles

MADE IN U.S.A.

Du Barry
GUARANTEED
PATTERNS

ILLUSTRATED INSTRUCTIONS for CUTTING and SEWING

ADVANCE PATTERNS
PARIS
LONDON
NEW YORK
PRINTED IN U.S.A.

25c
Advance
PATTERN

Dress and Bolero

2477

SIZE 16
Bust 34
Hip 37

Two
major
influences:

- **Wartime government order**
  limiting the amount of yardage
  a dress could use

- **Dior's New Look**

C H A P T E R F O U R

1940-1949

A Vogue 1940 retro pattern, re-sized for modern women.

Prepared especially for the readers of the
Woman's Home Companion

STYLE CHART FOR COMPANION-BUTTERICK PATTERN 9154
Shown on page 69 February issue Woman's Home Companion

Fabric -- "Baronette Crepe," fine all-worsted that will give splendid service. It is 54 inches wide, the price about $2.50 a yard. If your local stores do not carry this material they can specially order it for you from Botany Worsted Mills, Passaic, New Jersey.

Colors -- Newport Green -- one of the soft mossy tones, high style this spring. Dust Gold a flattering youthful tone of beige. Admiralty Blue -- as smart as ever, which means tops.

Style and Type -- An important dress for street wear, for traveling, for special daytime occasions. It is a woolen dress with soft lines, sure to hang beautifully because this fabric was in the designer's hands when she created the model.

What to Wear With It

Hat -- A small shape, not fluffy, not severe. The ribbon pillbox like that pictured in the February Companion, or one of these types, brown for the green; black for the beige; blue for the blue.

Gloves -- Simple pull-ons of washable suede or suede-surfaced cotton, in beige for the green; black or exactly matching beige for the gold; in white or bright red for the navy.

Bag -- A soft medium-large type in calf or kidskin, in brown for the green; black patent leather for the gold; blue for the blue.

Ribbon Bow -- Brown with green; black with gold; white with navy.

Jewelry -- One wide bracelet of gold or silver.

Shoes -- This dress calls for smart low-heeled town shoes. Here are three types, brown for the green; black for the gold; blue for the blue.

A style chart for Companion-Butterick pattern 9154.

1940-1949

Butterick
FASHION NEWS

August
1940

1077
See Back Cover

FOR A
Casual
SUMMER

1081   1068

BUTTERICK 1081. You see the buttons to the waist but the fly closing conceals them from there down. The tucks give a pulled in look to your waist. You'll like the big patch pockets, too. Size 16, 3⅝ yds. 36 in.; 1¾ yds. ribbon. Sizes 12 to 20; 30 to 46. Price, 45 cents.

BUTTERICK 1068. A buttoned closing on the shoulders is a new note on this tailored dress that is as trim as can be. The seams of the shaped panel are stitched. The skirt is in six pieces. Size 14, 3¾ yds. 36 in. linen. Junior Miss sizes 12 to 20; 30 to 38. Price, 45 cents.

2   Contents Copyrighted, 1940, United States and Great Britain by The Butterick Co., Inc.

BUTTERICK 9224. A flat shoulder line looks new on a casual dress and is accented by the shirring on the sleeve; this comes to point at the slash of yoke. There are gathers at each end of the slashes. Size 16, 3⅞ yds. 36 in. Designed for sizes 14 to 20; 32 to 40. Price, 15 cents.

BUTTERICK 9223. The pockets at the square yoke on this shirtwaist frock are stitched at the top and hang free. There is some fullness below the yoke in back. The skirt is in six pieces. Size 14, 3½ yds. 36 in.; ⅜ yd. 35 in. contrast. Jr. Miss sizes 10 to 18; 28 to 36. 15 cts.

BUTTERICK 1071. A dress that's as correct as it is casual. The belt is inserted in front, but loose in back, and ties in a bow. The seams are in saddle stitching. The skirt is in four pieces with a pleat front and back. Size 16, 4¼ yds. 36 in. cotton. Designed for 12 to 20; 30 to 44. 25 cents.

3

BUTTERICK 9230. The long torso in a two-piece dress with a contrasting front. The four gored skirt is on a band at natural waistline. Size 16, 3¾ yds. 36 in.; ⅜ yd. for bodice front. Sizes 14 to 20; 32 to 40. Price, 15 cents.

BUTTERICK 1061. Tri-color bands on a long torso line jacket dress. Size 16, 3⅞ yds. 39 in. silk shantung; ½ yd. each for upper and middle band; ¼ yd for lower band. Designed for sizes 12 to 20, 30 to 42. Price, 50 cents.

BUTTERICK 1053. A bias fold tied at each side creates the Polonaise silhouette. Skirt has fullness on each side of inverted pleat in back. Size 14, 3⅜ yds. 39 in. For Junior Miss sizes 12 to 20; 30 to 38. Price, 50 cents.

4

BUTTERICK 1054. The long torso, slim skirt adapted from a French import two piece dress. Gathers from yoke are caught at the sides. For size 16, 4½ yds. 39 in. crepe. Designed for sizes 12 to 20; 30 to 40. Price, 50 cents.

BUTTERICK 9225. A ribbon band encircles the bodice and stops the fullness from the shoulders on a frock with the long torso line. Size 16, 3½ yds. 39 in.; 2 yds. 1¼ in. ribbon. Designed for sizes 14 to 20; 32 to 40. Price, 15 cents.

COMPANION-BUTTERICK 1050. A long fitted midriff dress made of very few pieces. The skirt is gathered in panels around the hips. For size 16, 3½ yds. 39 in. mesh. Designed for sizes 12 to 20; 30 to 44. Price, 25 cents.

1054   9225   1050

BACKS ARE BLOUSED

1062   1055

COMPANION-BUTTERICK 1062. A drawstring waist blouse; the top of a two-piece dress. Bodice has three tucks with a pocket in the bottom of one. Skirt has four pieces. Size 14, 1¾ yds. 36 in. linen, skirt; 1¾ yds. top. Jr. Miss sizes 12 to 20; 30 to 38. Price, 25 cents.

COMPANION-BUTTERICK 1055. A slim skirt and bloused back dress with bishop sleeves. The front has a bias fold sewed on each side; large pockets with three buttons are allowed in skirt seams. Size 14, 4 yds. 39 in. Jr. Miss sizes 12 to 20; 30 to 38. Price, 45 cents.

1048   1079   1069

COMPANION-BUTTERICK 1048. The rolled collar, rounded yoke having fullness below it, and bloused back are all new on this spectator sports dress. One large button fastens the bodice. Size 16, 3½ yds. 36 in. cotton. For sizes 12 to 20; 30 to 44. Price, 45 cents.

BUTTERICK 1079. The big white collar on this dress has tiny circular inserts to make it ripple. The center panel of skirt is one with the bodice. The back of bodice is bloused. Size 16, 3½ yds. 39 in.; 1 yd. 36 in. collar and cuffs. Sizes 12 to 20; 30 to 44. Price, 50 cents.

BUTTERICK 1069. The striped vestee and sleeves give a guimpe effect to a sports dress which has the bloused back so popular now. The seams of bodice and six piece skirt are stitched. Size 16, 3½ yds. 36 in.; ½ yd. contrast. Sizes 12 to 20; 30 to 46. Price, 45 cents.

STARS TO SHINE FOR SUMMER NIGHTS

1067

1064-B

1064-A

9229

1084

BUTTERICK 1064-A. For rhumba rhythms, a lace cape and a full skirt. Size 14, 5¾ yds. 39 in.; 3 yds. 36 in. lace; ½ yd. net for cape foundation. Jr. Miss sizes 12 to 20; 30 to 38. 50¢.

BUTTERICK 9229. Little bows and shirring on the seam of a graduation or party dress. Size 14, 4¾ yds. 45 in.; 1¾ yds. edging; 2½ yds. ribbon. Jr. Miss 10 to 18; 28 to 36. 15¢.

BUTTERICK 1084. Wear a jacket tied with bows over a formal dress that's easy-to-sew. Size 14, 7¾ yds. 36 in. pique. In Junior Miss sizes 12 to 20; 30 to 38. Price, 25 cents.

1057   9220   9228

BUTTERICK 1057. Sunburst tucks on the bosom of an afternoon dress and a jabot forming a flower are feminine and pretty. The skirt is in three pieces. Size 16, 3¾ yds. 39 in. chiffon; ¾ yd. 45 in. organdie. Sizes 12 to 20; 30 to 42. Price, 50 cts.

BUTTERICK 9220. The fullness of a shaped yoke frames a wide neckline on an afternoon dress. The bodice buttons to waist and is bloused slightly. Skirt has soft unpressed pleats. Size 16, 3¾ yds. 39 in. Sizes 14 to 20; 32 to 40. 15 cents.

BUTTERICK 9228. A wide white collar with fullness at its sides on a frock opening to the waist. The skirt is in five pieces with unpressed pleats in front. Size 36, 3¾ yds. 39 in. voile; ½ yd., collar. Designed for sizes 36 to 44. Price, 15 cents.

BUTTERICK 1063. Princess dress adapted from the French with seams curved under the bosom releasing four sprays of fullness. Wide cuffs are important. Size 16, 4½ yds. 39 in. heavy sheer. Designed for sizes 12 to 20; 30 to 44. Price, 50 cents.

BUTTERICK 1085. Mesh makes a cool afternoon dress with a wide neck shirred at the sides. Fullness is caught into curved slashes above the waist. Skirt has three gores in back, two in front. Size 16, 3¾ yds. 39 in. 12 to 20; 30 to 44. 50 cts.

1063

1085

10

BUTTERICK 1073. A large white bow at the point of the wide neckline frames your throat becomingly. This has the new saddle shoulder with fullness just below. Size 16, 3⅝ yds. 39 in.; 1⅜ yds. ribbon. Sizes 12 to 20; 30 to 46. 25 cents.

COMPANION-BUTTERICK 1059. Await a blessed event in an adjustable back frock and sleeveless bolero jacket. Dress is expertly designed to hide an enlarging figure. Size 16, 4¾ yds. 39 in. plain; ¼ yd. 36, collar. 12 to 20; 30 to 42. 50 cts.

1073

1059

12

BUTTERICK 1088. Get a feeling of slimness and height in this dress with redingote effect. The inverted pleat and revers are trimmed by stitching. Size 38, 4½ yds. 36 in. linen. For shorter women of larger hip, 34 to 52. Price, 50 cents.

BUTTERICK 1074. Create an illusion of added inches and slimness in this dress with a soft lingerie collar and eight-gored skirt. Size 38, 4¾ yds. 36 in.; ½ yd., collar; 3⅜ yds. edging. For shorter women of larger hip, 34 to 52. Price, 50 cents.

BUTTERICK 1052. The surplice bodice and pleats all facing one way give the effect of a coat dress. Back of skirt is plain. The three-quarter length sleeve is good. Size 38, 4½ yds. 39 in. sheer crepe. In women's sizes 34 to 52. Price, 50 cents.

13

Pattern on the Cover

BUTTERICK 1077. Box pleats on the bodice and front of skirt of a sports dress. Stick a bunch of flowers in the belt that's stitched at waistline. Size 16, 4½ yds. 39 in. Sizes 12 to 20; 30 to 46. Price, 45 cts.

BUTTERICK 1083. Buttons down the sleeves give variety to a classic shirtwaist dress. Belt passes through loops. Skirt is in six pieces. Size 16, 3¼ yds. 35 in. Designed for sizes 12 to 20; 30 to 44. Price, 25 cents.

BUTTERICK 9226. The detail of unpressed pleats in the skirt is repeated with darts at waist and shoulders in a simple dress. Size 16, 3½ yds. 35 in. cotton; 1⅝ yds. ribbon. Sizes 14 to 20; 32 to 40. 15 cts.

Printed in U.S.A.

1940-1949

Lucille Ball on a Hollywood pattern.

An hourglass figure circa 1940.

A rare dated Simplicity pattern.

NO. S-4279—$1.00   SIZE 14
                                    32 BUST 35 HIP

*Vogue
Special
Design*

VOGUE
Vintage
MODEL

ORIGINAL
1940 DESIGN

DESSIN ORIGINAL
DE 1940

A,B

B

A

V1011
PATTERN/PATRON
SIZE/TAILLE
A (6-8-10)

2136   BUST   SIZE
                    36   18

25c

Butterick

B

A

A

McCall's pattern with background in illustration.

#4007
30" - 46" bust
$23.00

Decades of Style
PATTERN COMPANY

1940s New England Dress

Another retro pattern, circa 1940.

Simplicity 15¢ Pattern
GUARANTEED – CUT TO EXACT SIZE

4067

Size 12
Bust 30

Simple to Make

3

1

Simplicity is AMERICA'S FASHION

Size 16

8171

Prize
AND ECONOMY

CHARMING PAJAMA SET

A very feminine pajama set - something different and clever. You will like the high-waisted, form-fitting lines, the easy fulness across the back and over the bust. You will like the little girl charm of pert puffed sleeves, the dainty touch of lace edging the deep round yoke and sleeves. The pajama trousers are cut long and comfortably, can be made with a side-button placket or elastic across the back.

Please write us your re...

A Du Barry PERFECT PATTERN · 15¢   5245

Size 12
Bust 30

Early-Made

25¢

2

3

MADE IN U.S.A.

A rare dated DuBarry pattern.

15c SIZE 20 38 BUST
41 HIP
903

RENEE HAAL
OF RKO-RADIO

HOLLYWOOD PATTERN

HOLLYWOOD
Four Star
PATTERNS
25c

1287   SIZE 12 30 BUST
33 HIP

HOLLYWOOD PATTERN

Butterick begins using color in their illustrations.

3071　　BUST 36 SIZE 18

BUTTERICK 50c

. MAKE SURE SIZE IS CORRECT BEFORE OPENING

A　　B

FINDINGS 1132

1132　15c SIZE 18　36 BUST　39 HIP

JUNE HAVOC OF RKO-RADIO

HOLLYWOOD PATTERN

3　　2　　1

© THE H. P. CO.

Hollywood pattern when they no longer had movie star photos.

McCall
PRINTED PATTERN

B

Ladies' & Misses' Skirt or Jumper

5583

SIZE	WAIST
14	26½

35¢

A

McCall
PRINTED PATTERN

A

Misses' Dress

5598

SIZE	BUST
16	34

25¢

35¢

Advance Pattern

3952

SIZE 16
BUST 34
HIP 37

1

2

2

An Oriental motif.

McCALL
PRINTED PATTERN with TRANSFER

S600 · 20-Sears Roebuck and Co.
#1019 S24 N. E. Grand Avenue, Portland, Oregon

50¢

#20

A

*The Apron folded
for pressing*

B

Ladies' & Misses'
Necktie Apron
Trade Mark

Very new and fetching.
The accordion effect
comes from the narrow
sections shaped like a
man's necktie. When
made of striped mate-
rial, the bias sections
turn the stripes into
pretty zig-zag waves.
The sharp seam edges
are obtained by the
final pressing over
all folded sections.

884

ONE SIZE

BLUE OR YELLOW

BLUE

25c

NO. S-4673—$1.00   SIZE 16
34 BUST 37 HIP

Vogue Special Design

⑨ Pl-1-2
$1.00   ND

©Vogue
Printed in U.S.A.

NO. 5106—75c   SIZE 16
34 BUST 37 HIP

VOGUE PATTERN

⑨ Pl-1-8
$1.50   ND

©Vogue
Printed in U.S.A.

4039   BUST 32 SIZE 14

BUTTERICK   25¢   35¢

McCall
PRINTED PATTERN

6495
SIZE 16
BUST 34
Ladies' & Misses' Two-Piece Suit Dress
45c

McCall
PRINTED PATTERN

6589
SIZE 15
BUST 33
Junior Dress
50c

867   15¢   **SIZE 14** 32 BUST 35 HIP

HOLLYWOOD PATTERNS
TRADE MARK REG. U. S. PAT. OFF.

Instructions for crocheting detail are included in this pattern.

© THE H. P. CO.

3748

BUTTERICK 50c

BUST 34 SIZE 16

3107

Slacks or trousers were becoming accepted wear for women.

Typical wartime austerity — no fabric was wasted in frills.

The boxy, big-shouldered look was popular.

A. Pattern

4168

SIZE 18
BUST 36
HIP 39

1   2   3

McCall
PRINTED PATTERN

S 04

6010
Misses' Skirt
WAIST
28
35¢

McCall
PRINTED PATTERN

5320
SIZE
BUST
14
32
Ladies' & Misses' Housecoat
45¢

A

NO. 5339—75c

SIZE 18
36 BUST 39 HIP

VOGUE
PATTERN

©Vogue
Printed in U. S. A.

Note the color misprint on this Vogue.

35c   ADVANCE   4645

SIZE 14
Bust 32
Waist 26½

As Featured in
MADEMOISELLE

4783
SIZES
11-17

2173

Glove
Size 7

Simplicity PRINTED *Pattern* 25c

DETAILS PRINTED ON EACH PATTERN PIECE

2

3

1

4

5

Copyright by
Simplicity Pattern Co., Inc.

Simplicity IS AMERICA'S FASHION

McCall
PRINTED PATTERN

5986

Ladies' & Misses' Cape

SIZE 16
BUST 34

45c

A

B

C

McCall
PRINTED PATTERN

5968
WAIST 24
Misses' Skirt
35¢

(9) PO-12-4
$1.50

McCall
PRINTED PATTERN

6667
WAIST 26
Ladies' & Misses' Skirt
35¢

Misses' Aprons

Mon Mother
#20
50¢

McCALL
PRINTED PATTERN

1312
ONE SIZE
25¢

A

B

C

A 1946 Butterick retro pattern, re-sized for modern women.

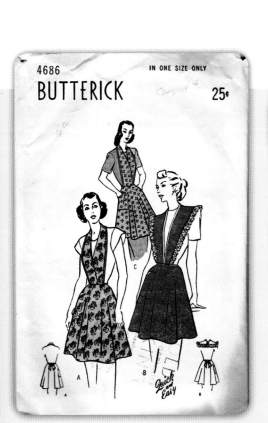

In 1977 my mother made me a dress from this circa 1947 pattern.

McCall
PRINTED PATTERN

25¢

A

B

NEW SLEEVE CONSTRUCTION*
*PATENT APPLIED FOR

7007
Misses Blouse
SIZE 14
BUST 34

45c

NO. 8472—30c   27 WAIST 35 HIP

VOGUE
PATTERN

B

B

A

PRINTED IN U. S. A.   ©Vogue

1940-1949

SIMPLICITY 2523 — Misses' One-Piece Dress in sizes 12, 14, 16, 18, 20. Size 16, Style 1: 4⅜ of 35″, 4 of 39″ or 2⅞ of 54″ even plaid or plain material. Bow: 1 yard of ½″ width ribbon. Style 2: 4¼ of 35″; 4 of 39″ or 41″ material. Width around lower edge of dress about 93″.   **Printed Pattern 25c**

2523 WITH DETAILS PRINTED ON EACH PATTERN PIECE

Simplicity IS AMER

127

2699 WITH DETAILS PRINTED ON EACH PATTERN PIECE

2699

128

2700 WITH DETAILS PRINTED ON EACH PATTERN PIECE

2700

The "Waistline"

Elegance

Eye For

401 — The woman of discernment will not want to overlook these reassuring lines that know where to go. This important dress offers a new way to achieve that slender waist by the diagonal cut of line through waist and over hip. Fitting climax to its smartness is the one-sided drape pouch, giving the appearance of being looped through, falling carelessly into sash.

401 — La dama elegante no querrá pasar por alto a este vestido con su distinguidas líneas. Pues ofrece un modo de obtener una cintura esbelta por el corte diagonal que pasa por la cintura y sobre la cadera. Una nota dominante acentúa aún más lo sencillo, es la bolsa drapeada en un lado, que da la apariencia de ser la terminación de una faja.

414 — An integral part of your wardrobe is this talented suit, enhanced by the rounded capelet shoulder over long sleeve. Rounded padded look achieved by pertinent cut over hip. Shadow-slim skirt.

414 — Este precioso trajecito con hombros extendidos y mangas largas formará una parte integral de su colección de vestidos. La apariencia redondeada se obtiene por medio de su corte original. La falda es recta y esbelta.

415 — Show up your figure to advantage in this exquisite creation. High-rounded neckline, criss-cross and a bit of peek-a-boo. Skirt with narrow, graduated peplum across and down.

415 — Su silueta obtendrá el efecto deseado con esta exquisita creación. La línea del cuello alta y redondeada, tiras que se cruzan y graciosas aberturas. La falda luce un novedoso peplo, atravéz y hacia abajo.

In 1948, Dior's New Look significantly impacted fashions: skirts were longer, and either very full or very slim, and the waist was accentuated

Contemporary Classics

406 — Tailored lines with a special talent for individuality . . . something for you to consider! Crisp, cool and SO American. Simple, rounded, notched collar, picked up by set-in contrast front that is top-stitched to reveal front flap over bust.

406 — Las líneas son puramente clásicas pero se prestan para hacer destacar cualquiera originalidad. Delicado, fresco y tan de moda. El sencillo cuello redondeado de muesca hace resaltar el corte delantero que esta sobrepespunteado y luce una tapa sobre el pecho.

407 — Your idea of style was never more beautifully embodied than by this more than slightly knock-out look. These are beautiful lines, to be dedicated to your own figure!

407 — Seguramente es este su idea de un vestido elegante y el que Ud. andaba buscando. Las bellas líneas del traje harán resaltar la esbeltez de su figura.

406

407

408 — Another classic co... reflect a new slant on this... It's angular in design, it... air, it's expensive to the... expensive to make.

408 — Otro traje clásico q... nueva tendencia de la mod... es singular, refleja una e... seada, de mucho lujo per... de hacer.

409 — Modern, sure an... straight, slender and sem... continues right through wa... ...vely minimizing hip. An id... of a dress to be cherished.

409 — Moderno, dramático... rectas, esbeltas y delicada... se concentra en la cintura p... la cadera. Un vestido idea... irresistible.

408

409

MODES ROYALE

416 — The charm of yesterday is presented for you today. It's the new, low-rounded neckline with low-slung double collar caught up at side with a rose. The skirt is soft and gentle, whispering echoes of the new you!

416 — El encanto de antaño reaparece en el presente. Se halla en el escote bajo y redondeado con un gracioso doble cuello que termina en un lado con una rosa. La falda es delicada y gentil para alegrar á todo corazón.

417 — The tailored and dressy are here smartly combined. A tuxedo-collared one-button jacket nipped in at waist. Draped front apron. Gay print is contrasted with pastel satin lapels.

417 — Aquí se combina con un encanto irresistible el traje sastre y el de más vestir. El cuello estilo smoking de la chaqueta con un botón es ideal. El delantal delantero está drapeado. La tela estampada hace contraste con las solapas de satín pálido.

416

417

After-Dark Drama

437 — Sculptured lines, dedicated to your own figure. Dramatically squared picture-frame neckline that laps over softly at front. Note unusual treatment of the peg-and-gathered skirt.

437 — Líneas esculturales ideal para su figura. El escote cuadrado dramáticamente enmarca su rostro. Fíjese en el original arreglo de la falda drapeada.

438 — You'll have the whole town in a whirl in this saucy, provocative number. Fitted bodice and bouffant skirt that offers delightful charm in the saucy, new, caught-up drape of the panniers.

438 — Llamará la atención por dondequiera que vaya con este elegante y provocativo vestido. El corpiño entallado y la falda amplia ofrece un delicioso encanto al combinarse con el atado drapeado.

Season's Spices

422 — New bold lines in asymmetric design further emphasized by contrasting materials of solids and stripes. Wonderfully wearable in your daily, active life.

422 — Unas atrevidas líneas acentúan el perfecto diseño de este traje que resalta aún más al confeccionarse con tela sólida haciendo contraste con la de rayas. Muy práctico para todos los días.

423 — Saucy and sophisticated triple-petal cowl-cadence neck with hug-me-tight bodice; full-swing skirt with set-in, contrasting, pleated front.

423 — Atractivo y elegante cuello de triple pétalos en el cuello alto y su corpiño bien ceñido; amplísima falda con vuelo con la parte delantera insertada y haciendo contraste.

MODES ROYA

424—Proclaim your man
erence for that different
your new silhouette. The
charm of yesterday is cl
terpreted here in the bac
of this bodice and doub

424 — Haga que su silhuet
taque por lo más nuevo y
El encanto del corse de
se ha prestado para form
terés del corpiño y la dob
de este lindo modelo.

425 — Center your interes
classic and be the center
est. A designer's subtle un
ment of crisp, simple lin
lighted with set-in, con
bands to pronounce foca
of interest.

425 — Al adquirir est
trajecito clásico será Ud.
de atracción. La perspe
ción del diseñador hac
la sencillez de su diseño
sus líneas como las m
hacienda contrasta

Interesting details on these artistic Modes Royale dresses.

Breadth of Fashion

429 — Frankly elegant under night lights in this number. Note the utter restraint in cut of front with all the drama surprisingly concentrated in back. The peg pouch flounce slit in back reveals contrasting skirt. Incidentally dots and solids are a must.

429 — Resulta ideal bajo las románticas luces de noche. La sencillez del corte delantero hace resaltar el interés que se ha concentrado en la parte de atrás. La ranura del volante trasero permite ver la falda contrastante. De paso manifestamos que las motitas y colores sólidos se llevan la supremacía.

430 — Swish floorward in a full swing skirt with a double flounce hem. Figure-flattering bodice with charming, softly gathered shoulder sleeve that falls into low back collar. Wonderful for After-Five frivolities.

430 — Baile alegremente en una falda con amplio vuelo y doble volante en el dobladillo. El corpiño moldea el cuerpo con unas adorables mangas cortas fruncidas que terminan en un cuello bajo en la parte de atrás. Perfecto para las citas después de las cinco.

429

430

Ballet Lengths

— Look that new way in this suit that
are expensive but is inexpensive to make,
offers much activity in its many fan-
ted inserts. Good tailoring and good lines
their own here.

— Para estar de moda nada más apro-
o. Escoja este traje que resulta tan caro
comprar pero tan económico para hacer,
falda ofrece en tan económico para hacer,
rriosos pliegues insertados.

— The new silhouette speaks a language
ts own! — Tapered to perfection in this
tail suit. Basic lines of a dinner vestón,
rpreted to a grand manner.

— La nueva silueta queda bien marcada
e lindo traje. Idéalo para resaltar por

431 — Put your pride in your
pocket, add an exciting fabric,
pick that fabric note up in lining
of voluminous swing skirt, and
retain the simple lines of a background dress, and you have dis-
tinction. It can belong to you!

431 — Arriba con su orgullo, con-
feccionado en una tela de fantasía,
que hace resaltar el amplio vuelo
de la falda y sin embargo muestra
las sencillas líneas de este elegante vestido, para hacer destacar su
persona!

432 — Splendor revisited in re-
fined lines that support basic com-
fort. You can be the fashion in
this classic print. Set-in front
panel controls just enough fullness over bustline. Simple, angular neckline; full-swing low-
dipping skirt.

432 — El resplendor de unas deli-
cadas líneas se muestran en este
sencillo trajecito. Siempre estará
de moda al confeccionarlo en tela
estampada. El insertado paño delantero moldea la figura. La línea
del cuello es interesantísima y
sencilla; la falda amplia y larga.

404 — The suit that i
diminutive lines. The s
formal look to the colla
the double-entry hip in
with the new ballerin
you have a top Modes

404 — El traje ha sid
unas líneas sencillas.
una nota nueva y aleg
Es el traje que se cono
interés en la cadera. El
nueva falda estilo bail

405 — A new, bold cu
achieved in this suit b
recommendation of t
jacket, set off by bu
points. It falls into st
the front waistline. Se
skirt goes to new lengh

405 — Una nueva creac

Study in Contour

410 — A little treasure to be cherished. High-button suit with crisp mandarin neckline. Cuffed pushup sleeve. Full and carefree skirt.

410 — Un tesoro que apreciará con todo su corazón. Traje elegante abotonado en alto con un escote estilo mandarín. Las mangas recogidas y con puños. La falda es amplia y graciosa.

411 — Sleek, gracious and sweeping is this delightful satin dance frock for afternoon or evening. Picture-frame neckline, flattering to any figure. Off-the-shoulder drape sweeps around the back. Softly rounded at hip.

411 — Elegante, gracioso y de sumo orgullo resulta este traje de baile en satén para las tardes o fiestas nocturnas. El escote enmarca la cara a la vez que moldea la figura. El drapeado caído del hombro llega hasta la parte de atrás. El efecto de las caderas es redondo.

MODES ROYALE

439 — You are the fashion in this exquisite translation of this season's silhouette. Dramatic lace yoke-collar . . . just-right button-down waist jacket, rounded and front-draped.

439 — Estará de moda con esta linda creación de la silueta más popular de la temporada. El cuello canesú es de encaje . . . la chaqueta se abotona realizando el redondeado drapeado delantero.

440 — Lean, long lines of elegance over front bodice and skirt that is contrasted by a cloud of airiness, flaring in rippling fantasy. Figure is further glorified by contrasting print lining.

440 — Las largas esbeltas líneas realzan la elegancia del corpiño delantero y la falda a la vez que hace contraste con el nubloso cuello amplio. La silueta se destaca aún más si confeccionarse con un forro en tela estampada.

412 — Balance is the keynote to
design. Here this theme is accente
a perky, pleated ruffle bordering
line, and triple hip flange at th
of an otherwise simple skirt.

412 — Bien proporcionado es la
la clave de buen diseño. Aquí se
su importancia por medio de u
lantes plegados en el escote, y la
ringleras en las caderas de l
sencilla.

413 — Note how the cut of our
always achieves sophistication
does not depart from awareness
ure requirements. Here is a
example. Bold and dramatic,
material is classically draped
side.

413 — Fíjese como nuestros
siempre son de última moda y
halagan sumamente a la figura.
tamos un perfecto ejemplo con
je. Esbelto y dramático con l
motitas formando un drapead
lado.

412   *413*

Traditionally Sentimental

445 — The bride pre-
sents a fantasy of love-
liness, exquisitely swath-
ed in yards of gentle
drapery. The lines are
simple, but oh, so know-
ing. Note the bare look
injected in the high,
rounded neckline yoke
and three-quarter sleeve.
Waist is whittled, fall-
ing low and rounded at
hip flounce.

445 — La novia presenta
un cuadro de una be-
lleza fantástica, primo-
rosamente envuelta en
metros de delicada tela.
Las líneas son sencillas
pero de atracción única.
Fíjese en la sugestiva
línea del cuello alto y
redondeado y las man-
gas de tres cuartos. La
cintura queda bien en-
tallada cayendo bajo y
redondeado en los vo-
lantes de la cadera.

446 — The demureness
of the bridesmaid echoes
the loveliness of the
bride. A treasure to be
cherished is this well-
turned-out and thought-
out design.

446 — La belleza de la
madrina de boda refleja
el encanto de la novia.
Un tesoro irresistible resulta este precioso traje
tan cuidadosamente di-
señado e ideado.

445   *446*

1940-1949

BUTTERICK
Fashion News
AUGUST 1948

"SIZED TO HEIGHT"
PATTERNS
For Women Under 5'5"

If you are under 5'5", Butterick "Sized to Height" patterns elim- inate time-consuming and com- plicated length adjustments. Full details on page two.

New Styles Every Month

4610

Description on page 5

DO YOU KNOW

BUTTERICK HAS A SPECIAL PATTERN SERVICE FOR WOMEN UNDER 5'5"?

Butterick "Sized to Height" patterns for women under 5'5" are proportioned to eliminate time-consuming and fre- quently complicated length adjust- ments. Other proportions of these special length patterns conform in every way with standard measure- ments. If you are under 5'5" and your figure is of average proportions, you will find that Butterick "Sized to Height" patterns will save you both time and money as they require less fabric than standard length patterns. * On these pages patterns 4606, 4586, 4538, 4575, 4599 and 4571 are available in two lengths: Special length for fig- ures under 5'5"; Standard length for figures 5'5" and over. When ordering Special length patterns add the letter S to the pattern number.

* 4606 — Butterick. The casual is calm, cool and charming for torrid days. Curved kimono sleeves harmonize with revers and pockets on the flared skirt. Size 16. Standard length, 4⅛ yds. 35 in.; Special, 3⅞ yds Misses 12-20. 50¢.

* 4586 — Butterick. Very chic, very gay, very dashing all the way . . . the Gibson Girl dress with flared skirt. Size 16. Standard length, 3½ yds. 39 in.; Special length, 3¼ yds. Each, ⅜ yd. 35 in. contrast. Misses, 12-20, 30-38. 50¢.

* 4538 — Butterick. Toss a stole over your shoulders and go to the smartest places this Summer. We think this stole-dress is a fashion "must". Size 16. Standard, 3⅝ yds 39"; Special 3½ yds. Each 1 yd. for stole. Misses 12-20. 50¢.

* 4575 — Butterick Swirl-skirted casual with unpressed pleats adds to its billowing silhou- ette. Cap sleeves are cut in one with the bod- ice. Size 16. Standard length, 4½ yds. 35 in.; Special length, 4¼ yds. Misses 12-20, 30-38. 50¢.

* 4599 — Butterick. A dress that so aptly com- bines an urban flair with a suburban air. Full skirt has inverted pleats either side in front. Size 16. Standard length, 3½ yds. 39 in. Spe- cial length 3¼ yds. Misses 12-20, 30-38. 50¢.

* 4571 — Butterick. For melting days in the city or traveling to the country, wear a two- piecer that features a saucy back-flare on its blouse top. Size 16. Standard, 5 yds. 35 in., Special length, 4¾ yds. Misses 12-20, 30-38. 50¢.

Copyright, 1948, by the Butterick Company, Inc. in the United States and Great Britain.

* 4606

2

* 4599   * 4571

* 4586

* 4538

* 4575

BLOUSES INSPIRE SUITS

Blouse 4604

4600

Blouse 4616B

Blouse 4616C

4601

4600 — Butterick. Long lissome jacket plus a slim skirt equals a stunning suit. Size 16, 4⅛ yds. 39 in.; 2¼ yds. ¾ in. braid trim. Misses' 12 to 20; 30 to 38. Price 50 Cents.

4604 — Butterick. Sleeves and yoke are cut in one on this softly tailored blouse. Note the dashing notched revers collar. Size 16, 1¾ yds. 39 in. Misses' 12 to 20; 30 to 38. 35 Cents.

4616B—Butterick. Yoke blouse with demure collar, cuff sleeves and button-back closing. Size 16, 2 yds. 39 in., ⅜ yd. 35in lace yoke. Misses' 12 to 20; 30 to 38. Price 35 Cents.

4601 — Butterick. Two-piece bolero suit. The short-sleeved jacket flares back so flippantly. Slim-skirt with front pleat. Size 16, 2⅛ yds. 54 in. 3¾ yds. braid. Misses' 12-20. 50 Cents.

4616C — Butterick. "Portrait" blouse lace-framing U neckline, puff sleeves with turndown cuffs, back buttoning. Size 16, 1⅜ yds. 39 in. Misses' 12 to 20; 30 to 38. 35 Cents.

TO PLAY MANY ROLES

4590

Blouse 4603

Blouse 4617

4617 — Butterick. Peter Pan collar shirt blouse classic has front buttoning, short sleeves and one patch pocket. Size 16, 1⅝ yds. 39 in. Sizes 12 to 20; 30 to 44. 35 Cents.

4590—Three-piece suit. Its box jacket swings over the bow blouse. Flare skirt has a corselet waist. Size 16, 3⅛ yds. 54 in.; blouse, 1¾ yds. 35 in., 2½ yds. insertion. Misses' 12-20. 50¢.

4603—Butterick. Kimono sleeved button-front blouse features a deep yoke and soft fulness in the back. See the saddle stitching. Size 16, 2¼ yds. 35 in. Misses' 12-20; 30-38. 35 Cents.

On The Front Cover

4610 — Butterick. Back fulness is fashion's newest feature interpreted here in a soft casual, yoke on bodice and skirt, kimono sleeves. Size 16, 5 yds. 39 in. Misses 12-20. 50¢.

FLUID SKIRTED CASUALS

4605

4597A

4597B

4610

4597

4605—Butterick. There's a delightful ingenue air about this newest version of the ever-beloved shirtwaister. A ruffle outlines the yoke tucked in front, plain in back. Unpressed pleats add fulness to the skirt. Size 16, 6½ yds. 35 in. Misses' 12 to 20; 30 to 38. 50 Cents.

4610—Butterick. The casual gets top billing for its versatility. Cap sleeves are cut in one with the bodice; waistline is cinched-in; a curved yoke accents back fulness on the flared skirt. Yoke in back of the bodice, too. Size 16, 4¾ yds. 35 in. Misses 12-20; 30-38. 50¢.

4597 — Butterick. Soft-tailored flare-skirted frock. (A) Contrasting detachable collar and cuffs . . . and a smart button-on cape collar. Size 16, 4⅜ yds. 35 in., ½ yd. contrast. (B) 3⅜ yds. 39 in. Sizes 12 to 20; 30 to 42. 50¢.

7

"WHIRL LINES" FOR TEENERS

4611

4612

4613

4614

4612 — Butterick. "Fair flair" a casual new topic for teeners. Don't forget to look at the very different neckline! Size 14, 4½ yds. 35 in. Teen Age 12 to 18; 30 to 36. Price, 25 Cents.

4614 — Butterick. Swagger smoothie for a sweet teener . . . boxy flare-back jacket with big cuffs and a slim skirt make such a smart suit. Size 14 4½ yds. 39". Teen Age 10-16; 28-34. 50¢.

4613—Butterick. Suited for year 'round wear, fitted jacket with little girl collar and fullish skirt with unpressed pleats. Size 14, 2½ yds. 39 in. jacket, 2 yds. skirt. 10 to 16; 28 to 34. 50¢.

4611 — Butterick. Bewitching date bait, the jacket dress . . . bare-top, flare-skirt dress worn 'neath the fitted rippling peplum jacket! Size 14, 4½ yds. 39 in. 12 to 18; 30 to 36. 35¢.

6

4592

4598

4593

4615

4574

4608

9

10 WOMEN'S FLARED FASHIONS

4589—Butterick. Purpose of this dress is "flattery for women". Look at the graceful curve of its surplice bodice accented by the narrow collar; the soft sleeves in (A); the contrast collar and tailored cuff sleeves in (B); and the flared skirt. Size 36, (A) 4⅛ yds. 39, (B) 3⅞ yds. 39 in., ⅞ yd. contrast. Sizes 34 to 44. 50¢.

4581—Butterick. A dress designed to fuse character with charm during every hour of the day. Capelet sleeves ripple softly over the shoulders . . . the bodice buttons up to a high round neckline . . . the four-gore flared skirt is topped by a tiny V-shaped yoke in the front. Size 36, 4 yds. 39 in. Sizes 34 to 48. Price 50c.

4579—Butterick. The cape dress for the woman with smart new ideas about fashion. The deep cape collar falls softly about the shoulders and crosses over in a surplice line. Its six-gore skirt flares gently as you walk. The dress is "Quick & Easy" to cut and to sew. Size 36, 4¼ yds. 39 in. Sizes 34 to 46. Price, 50 Cents.

ENCHANTED EVENING IN A GOWN THAT FLOWS OR BILLOWS!

4609—Butterick. Designed to dance rhythms . . . a two-piece dress of fluid grace with off-shoulder decolletage, wee waist and circular skirt. Shirr the blouse with elastic thread for a very interesting effect. "Quick and Easy" Size 16, 6⅜ yds. 39 in. Misses' 12-20; 30-38. 50¢.

4602—Butterick. Story book heroine dress as romantic as the summer stars. A pleated ruffle encircles the off-shoulder decolletage and a deep pleated flounce sweeps around the hemline of the billowing skirt. Size 16, 7¾ yds. 35", 2½ yds. 1" ribbon. Misses 12-20; 30-38. 50¢.

McCall
PRINTED PATTERN

7489
Misses' Blouse

SIZE 16
BUST 34

35c

McCall
PRINTED PATTERN

7183
Ladies' & Misses' Dress

SIZE 16
BUST 36

50c

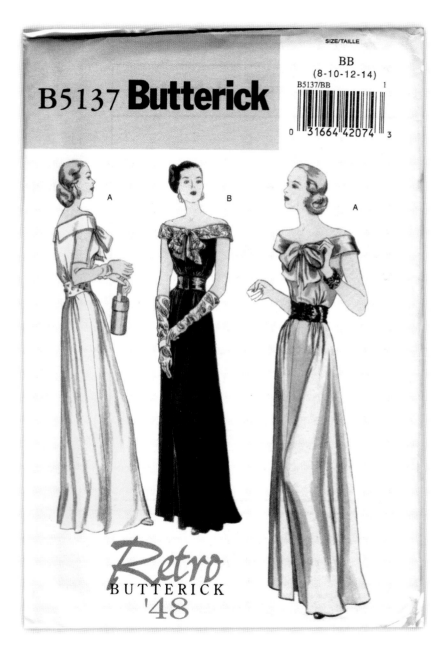

Butterick retro pattern from 1948.

Teenage fashions were a new subcategory.

25c **ADVANCE*** **4832**

SIZE 12
BUST 30
HIP 33

PREG. U. S. PAT. OFF.

1

2

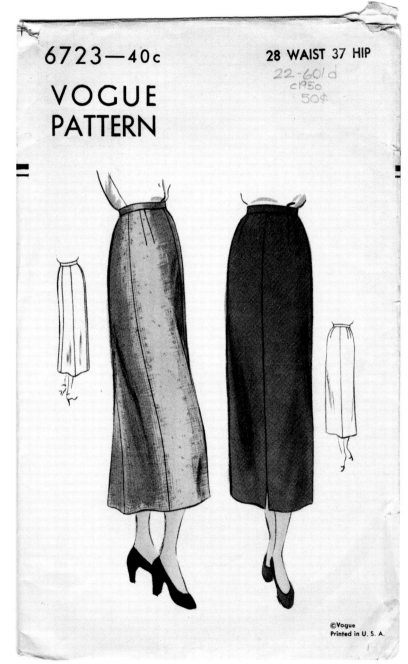

6723—40c 28 WAIST 37 HIP

22-601d
c1950
50¢

**VOGUE
PATTERN**

©Vogue
Printed in U. S. A.

McCall
PRINTED PATTERN

7541
Junior Dress

SIZE 17
BUST 35

35c

McCall
PRINTED PATTERN

7839
Misses' Vest

SIZE 16
BUST 34

35c

Weskits or vests enjoyed a brief popularity.

2836
Size 10
Bust 28

Simplicity PRINTED Pattern 25c

DETAILS PRINTED ON EACH PATTERN PIECE

Simple to Make

2878
Size 12
Bust 30

Simplicity PRINTED Pattern 25c

DETAILS PRINTED ON EACH PATTERN PIECE

Simplicity IS AMERICA'S FASHION

Copyright by
Simplicity Pattern Co.

2938
Size 14
Bust 32

Simplicity PRINTED Pattern 25c

DETAILS PRINTED ON EACH PATTERN PIECE

Copyright by
Simplicity Pattern Co., Inc.

Simplicity's TRULY TEEN STYLE

CHAPTER FIVE

1950-1959

A new Simplicity artist, or just a new style of drawing?

Circa 1954, a "truly teen" style.

1950-1959

Circa 1954, shoulders are de-accentuated.

4463
Size 16
Bust 34

35¢

Simplicity PRINTED *Pattern*

DETAILS PRINTED ON EACH PATTERN PIECE

1

2

Butterick
PRINTED
PATTERN

6017

BUST 34   SIZE 16

50¢

A

B

A maternity style.

The "wiggle" skirt.

1950-1959

Skirts are still full, but shorter.

Circa 1959, a very defined waist; slacks are slim.

Two
major
influences:

- Young English "mod" designers in the 1960s

- Princess Diana in the 1980s

CHAPTER SIX

Post-1959

Circa 1967, the "mod" look.

MISSES' DRESS IN TWO LENGTHS
AND PANTS

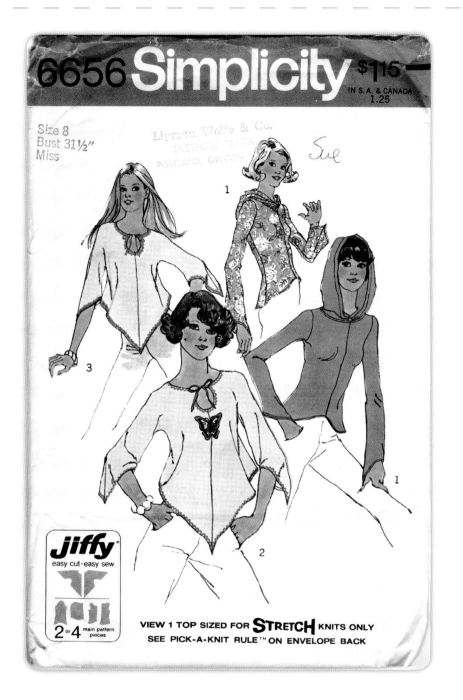

Circa 1977, the Farrah Fawcett look.

Post-1959

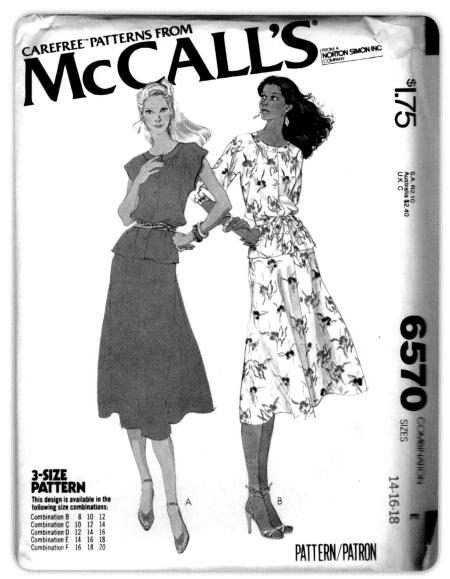

Circa 1980, very long legs.

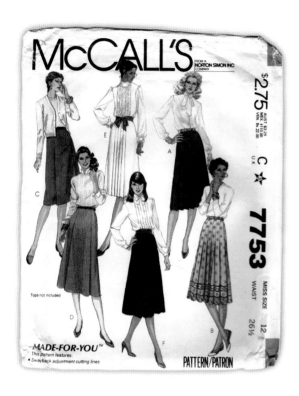

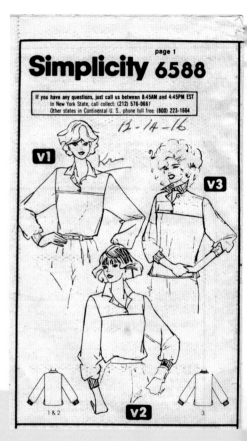

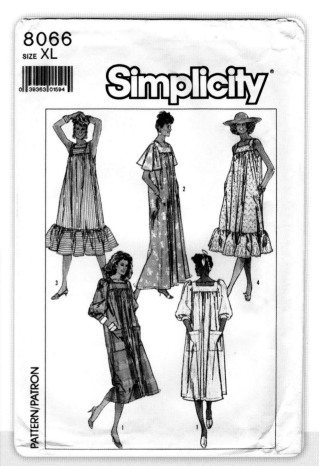

BUTTERICK®

3186
PATTERN/PATRON
SIZE/TAILLE

16

7705

H | 6+8+10
Eur | 34+36+38

Simplicity®

PATTERN/PATRON

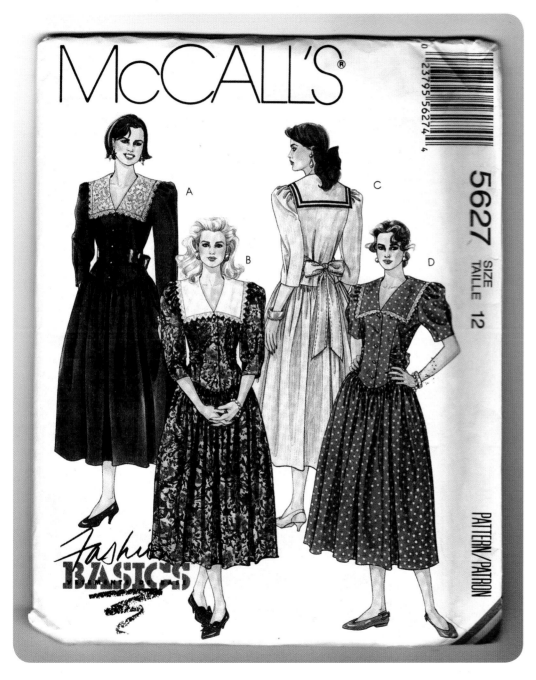

Circa 1994, a very "Victorian" dress.

FIDM Museum Blog. Los Angeles, California: Fashion
Institute of Design & Merchandising, 2010.
LaBoissonniere, Wade. *Blueprints of Fashion: Home
Sewing Patterns of the 1940s*. Atglen, Pennsylvania:
Schiffer Publishing Ltd., 2009.
Shoemaker, LouAnn. *Dress Patterns*. Chicago, Illinois:
Antiques & Collecting Magazine, 2010.

Other sources

www.Fashion-Era.com
www.VintageFashionGuild.org
www.wikipedia.org

BIBLIOGRAPH